THE EMPLOYMENT SITUATION — FEBRUARY 2015

Total **nonfarm payroll employment** increased by 295,000 in February, and the **unemployment rate** edged down to 5.5 percent, the U.S. Bureau of Labor Statistics reported today. Job gains occurred in food services and drinking places, professional and business services, construction, health care, and in transportation and warehousing. Employment in mining was down over the month.

Chart 1. Unemployment rate, seasonally adjusted, February 2013 – February 2015

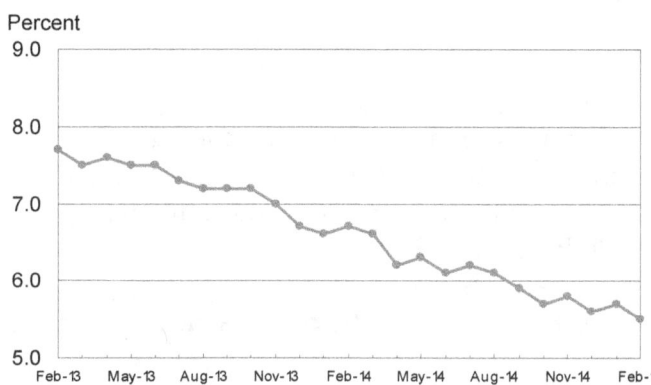

Chart 2. Nonfarm payroll employment over-the-month change, seasonally adjusted, February 2013 – February 2015

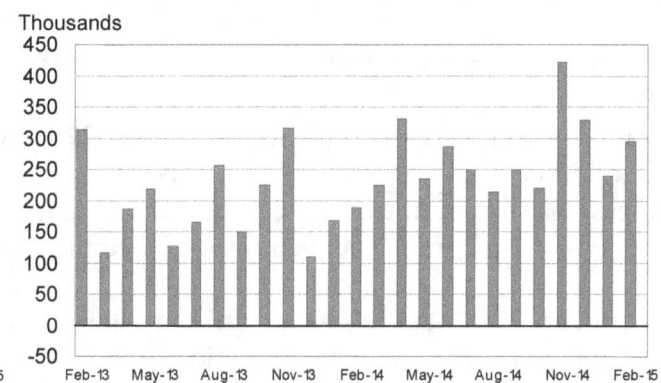

Household Survey Data

Both the **unemployment rate** (5.5 percent) and the number of **unemployed persons** (8.7 million) edged down in February. Over the year, the unemployment rate and the number of unemployed persons were down by 1.2 percentage points and 1.7 million, respectively. (See table A-1.)

Among the **major worker groups**, the unemployment rate for teenagers decreased by 1.7 percentage points to 17.1 percent in February. The jobless rates for adult men (5.2 percent), adult women (4.9 percent), whites (4.7 percent), blacks (10.4 percent), Asians (4.0 percent), and Hispanics (6.6 percent) showed little or no change. (See tables A-1, A-2, and A-3.)

The number of **long-term unemployed** (those jobless for 27 weeks or more) was little changed at 2.7 million in February. These individuals accounted for 31.1 percent of the unemployed. Over the past 12 months, the number of long-term unemployed is down by 1.1 million. (See table A-12.)

The **civilian labor force participation rate**, at 62.8 percent, changed little in February and has remained within a narrow range of 62.7 to 62.9 percent since April 2014. The **employment-population ratio** was unchanged at 59.3 percent in February but is up by 0.5 percentage point over the year. (See table A-1.)

The number of persons employed **part time for economic reasons** (sometimes referred to as involuntary part-time workers) was little changed in February at 6.6 million. These individuals, who would have preferred full-time employment, were working part time because their hours had been cut back or because they were unable to find a full-time job. (See table A-8.)

In February, 2.2 million persons were **marginally attached to the labor force**, little changed from a year earlier. (The data are not seasonally adjusted.) These individuals were not in the labor force, wanted and were available for work, and had looked for a job sometime in the prior 12 months. They were not counted as unemployed because they had not searched for work in the 4 weeks preceding the survey. (See table A-16.)

Among the marginally attached, there were 732,000 **discouraged workers** in February, little different from a year earlier. (The data are not seasonally adjusted.) Discouraged workers are persons not currently looking for work because they believe no jobs are available for them. The remaining 1.4 million persons marginally attached to the labor force in February had not searched for work for reasons such as school attendance or family responsibilities. (See table A-16.)

Establishment Survey Data

Total **nonfarm payroll employment** rose by 295,000 in February, compared with an average monthly gain of 266,000 over the prior 12 months. Job gains occurred in food services and drinking places, professional and business services, construction, health care, and in transportation and warehousing. Employment in mining declined over the month. (See table B-1.)

In February, **food services and drinking places** added 59,000 jobs. The industry had added an average of 35,000 jobs per month over the prior 12 months.

Employment in **professional and business services** increased by 51,000 in February and has risen by 660,000 over the year. In February, employment continued to trend up in management and technical consulting services (+7,000), computer systems design and related services (+5,000), and architectural and engineering services (+5,000).

Construction added 29,000 jobs in February. Employment in specialty trade contractors rose by 27,000, mostly in the residential component. Over the past 12 months, construction has added 321,000 jobs.

In February, employment in **health care** rose by 24,000, with gains in ambulatory care services (+20,000) and hospitals (+9,000). Health care had added an average of 29,000 jobs per month over the prior 12 months.

Transportation and warehousing added 19,000 jobs in February, with most of the gain occurring in couriers and messengers (+12,000). Employment in transportation and warehousing grew by an average of 14,000 per month over the prior 12 months.

Employment in **retail trade** continued to trend up in February (+32,000) and has grown by 319,000 over the year.

Manufacturing employment continued to trend up in February (+8,000). Within the industry, petroleum and coal products lost 6,000 jobs, largely due to a strike.

Employment in **mining** decreased by 9,000 in February, with most of the decline in support activities for mining (-7,000).

Employment in other major industries, including **wholesale trade**, **information**, **financial activities**, and **government**, showed little change over the month.

In February, the **average workweek for all employees** on private nonfarm payrolls was 34.6 hours for the fifth month in a row. The manufacturing workweek was unchanged at 41.0 hours in February, and factory overtime edged down by 0.1 hour to 3.4 hours. The average workweek for **production and nonsupervisory employees** on private nonfarm payrolls was unchanged at 33.8 hours. (See tables B-2 and B-7.)

In February, **average hourly earnings for all employees** on private nonfarm payrolls rose by 3 cents to $24.78. Over the year, average hourly earnings have risen by 2.0 percent. In February, average hourly earnings of private-sector **production and nonsupervisory employees** were unchanged at $20.80. (See tables B-3 and B-8.)

After revision, the change in total nonfarm payroll employment for December remained at +329,000, and the change for January was revised from +257,000 to +239,000. With these revisions, employment gains in December and January were 18,000 lower than previously reported. Over the past 3 months, job gains have averaged 288,000 per month.

_____

The Employment Situation for March is scheduled to be released on Friday, April 3, 2015, at 8:30 a.m. (EDT).

Summary table A. Household data, seasonally adjusted

[Numbers in thousands]

Category	Feb. 2014	Dec. 2014	Jan. 2015	Feb. 2015	Change from: Jan. 2015- Feb. 2015
Employment status					
Civilian noninstitutional population.............................	247,085	249,027	249,723	249,899	176
Civilian labor force..	155,688	156,129	157,180	157,002	-178
Participation rate..	63.0	62.7	62.9	62.8	-0.1
Employed..	145,301	147,442	148,201	148,297	96
Employment-population ratio...........................	58.8	59.2	59.3	59.3	0.0
Unemployed..	10,387	8,688	8,979	8,705	-274
Unemployment rate......................................	6.7	5.6	5.7	5.5	-0.2
Not in labor force...	91,398	92,898	92,544	92,898	354
Unemployment rates					
Total, 16 years and over..	6.7	5.6	5.7	5.5	-0.2
Adult men (20 years and over)...........................	6.3	5.3	5.3	5.2	-0.1
Adult women (20 years and over).......................	5.9	5.0	5.1	4.9	-0.2
Teenagers (16 to 19 years)................................	21.3	16.8	18.8	17.1	-1.7
White..	5.8	4.8	4.9	4.7	-0.2
Black or African American..................................	12.0	10.4	10.3	10.4	0.1
Asian..	5.9	4.2	4.0	4.0	0.0
Hispanic or Latino ethnicity...............................	8.1	6.5	6.7	6.6	-0.1
Total, 25 years and over..	5.4	4.5	4.6	4.5	-0.1
Less than a high school diploma.........................	9.8	8.6	8.5	8.4	-0.1
High school graduates, no college......................	6.4	5.3	5.4	5.4	0.0
Some college or associate degree......................	6.0	4.9	5.2	5.1	-0.1
Bachelor's degree and higher.............................	3.4	2.9	2.8	2.7	-0.1
Reason for unemployment					
Job losers and persons who completed temporary jobs..................	5,403	4,325	4,242	4,180	-62
Job leavers..	816	798	851	884	33
Reentrants...	2,972	2,701	2,829	2,655	-174
New entrants..	1,232	971	1,033	972	-61
Duration of unemployment					
Less than 5 weeks...	2,388	2,375	2,383	2,431	48
5 to 14 weeks...	2,558	2,293	2,318	2,223	-95
15 to 26 weeks...	1,597	1,274	1,380	1,335	-45
27 weeks and over..	3,804	2,785	2,800	2,709	-91
Employed persons at work part time					
Part time for economic reasons.............................	7,204	6,790	6,810	6,635	-175
Slack work or business conditions.......................	4,259	4,061	4,012	3,847	-165
Could only find part-time work.............................	2,674	2,432	2,460	2,426	-34
Part time for noneconomic reasons........................	19,085	19,730	19,822	19,837	15
Persons not in the labor force (not seasonally adjusted)					
Marginally attached to the labor force.....................	2,303	2,260	2,234	2,159	–
Discouraged workers..	755	740	682	732	–

- Over-the-month changes are not displayed for not seasonally adjusted data.

NOTE: Persons whose ethnicity is identified as Hispanic or Latino may be of any race. Detail for the seasonally adjusted data shown in this table will not necessarily add to totals because of the independent seasonal adjustment of the various series. Updated population controls are introduced annually with the release of January data.

ESTABLISHMENT DATA
Summary table B. Establishment data, seasonally adjusted

Category	Feb. 2014	Dec. 2014	Jan. 2015[p]	Feb. 2015[p]
EMPLOYMENT BY SELECTED INDUSTRY (Over-the-month change, in thousands)				
Total nonfarm...	188	329	239	295
Total private..	175	319	237	288
Goods-producing...	47	64	64	29
Mining and logging....................................	1	1	-6	-8
Construction..	26	44	49	29
Manufacturing..	20	19	21	8
Durable goods[1]......................................	17	14	16	11
Motor vehicles and parts...........................	12.5	2.2	3.8	0.8
Nondurable goods.....................................	3	5	5	-3
Private service-providing..............................	128	255	173	259
Wholesale trade.......................................	8.5	14.3	14.0	11.7
Retail trade..	-19.1	-0.2	27.8	32.0
Transportation and warehousing.....................	-3.7	38.4	1.0	18.5
Utilities...	-0.2	1.8	0.5	0.4
Information...	-4	6	5	7
Financial activities....................................	13	7	22	10
Professional and business services[1]................	69	72	10	51
Temporary help services............................	16.9	21.0	-13.8	-7.8
Education and health services[1]......................	30	54	46	54
Health care and social assistance.................	19.1	47.5	52.5	32.8
Leisure and hospitality................................	32	56	39	66
Other services...	2	6	7	9
Government...	13	10	2	7
(3-month average change, in thousands)				
Total nonfarm...	154	324	330	288
Total private..	161	317	323	281
WOMEN AND PRODUCTION AND NONSUPERVISORY EMPLOYEES **AS A PERCENT OF ALL EMPLOYEES**[2]				
Total nonfarm women employees...........................	49.4	49.3	49.3	49.3
Total private women employees...........................	47.9	47.9	47.8	47.8
Total private production and nonsupervisory employees...	82.6	82.5	82.5	82.5
HOURS AND EARNINGS **ALL EMPLOYEES** **Total private**				
Average weekly hours......................................	34.4	34.6	34.6	34.6
Average hourly earnings...................................	$24.30	$24.62	$24.75	$24.78
Average weekly earnings...................................	$835.92	$851.85	$856.35	$857.39
Index of aggregate weekly hours (2007=100)[3]...........	99.8	102.7	102.9	103.1
Over-the-month percent change.........................	0.2	0.3	0.2	0.2
Index of aggregate weekly payrolls (2007=100)[4]........	115.7	120.6	121.5	121.9
Over-the-month percent change.........................	0.5	0.0	0.7	0.3
DIFFUSION INDEX (Over 1-month span)[5]				
Total private (263 industries).............................	61.8	69.2	62.0	65.4
Manufacturing (80 industries).............................	55.0	64.4	61.3	64.4

[1] Includes other industries, not shown separately.

[2] Data relate to production employees in mining and logging and manufacturing, construction employees in construction, and nonsupervisory employees in the service-providing industries.

[3] The indexes of aggregate weekly hours are calculated by dividing the current month's estimates of aggregate hours by the corresponding annual average aggregate hours.

[4] The indexes of aggregate weekly payrolls are calculated by dividing the current month's estimates of aggregate weekly payrolls by the corresponding annual average aggregate weekly payrolls.

[5] Figures are the percent of industries with employment increasing plus one-half of the industries with unchanged employment, where 50 percent indicates an equal balance between industries with increasing and decreasing employment.

p Preliminary

NOTE: Data have been revised to reflect March 2014 benchmark levels and updated seasonal adjustment factors.

Frequently Asked Questions about Employment and Unemployment Estimates

1. Why are there two monthly measures of employment?

The household survey and establishment survey both produce sample-based estimates of employment, and both have strengths and limitations. The establishment survey employment series has a smaller margin of error on the measurement of month-to-month change than the household survey because of its much larger sample size. An over-the-month employment change of about 100,000 is statistically significant in the establishment survey, while the threshold for a statistically significant change in the household survey is about 400,000. However, the household survey has a more expansive scope than the establishment survey because it includes self-employed workers whose businesses are unincorporated, unpaid family workers, agricultural workers, and private household workers, who are excluded by the establishment survey. The household survey also provides estimates of employment for demographic groups. For more information on the differences between the two surveys, please visit www.bls.gov/web/empsit/ces_cps_trends.pdf.

2. Are undocumented immigrants counted in the surveys?

It is likely that both surveys include at least some undocumented immigrants. However, neither the establishment nor the household survey is designed to identify the legal status of workers. Therefore, it is not possible to determine how many are counted in either survey. The establishment survey does not collect data on the legal status of workers. The household survey does include questions which identify the foreign and native born, but it does not include questions about the legal status of the foreign born. Data on the foreign and native born are published each month in table A-7 of The Employment Situation news release.

3. Why does the establishment survey have revisions?

The establishment survey revises published estimates to improve its data series by incorporating additional information that was not available at the time of the initial publication of the estimates. The establishment survey revises its initial monthly estimates twice, in the immediately succeeding 2 months, to incorporate additional sample receipts from respondents in the survey and recalculated seasonal adjustment factors. For more information on the monthly revisions, please visit www.bls.gov/ces/cesrevinfo.htm.

On an annual basis, the establishment survey incorporates a benchmark revision that re-anchors estimates to nearly complete employment counts available from unemployment insurance tax records. The benchmark helps to control for sampling and modeling errors in the estimates. For more information on the annual benchmark revision, please visit www.bls.gov/web/empsit/cesbmart.htm.

4. Does the establishment survey sample include small firms?

Yes; about 40 percent of the establishment survey sample is comprised of business establishments with fewer than 20 employees. The establishment survey sample is designed to maximize the reliability of the statewide total nonfarm employment estimate; firms from all states, size classes, and industries are appropriately sampled to achieve that goal.

5. Does the establishment survey account for employment from new businesses?

Yes; monthly establishment survey estimates include an adjustment to account for the net employment change generated by business births and deaths. The adjustment comes from an econometric model that forecasts the monthly net jobs impact of business births and deaths based on the actual past values of the net impact that can be observed with a lag from the Quarterly Census of Employment and Wages. The establishment survey uses modeling rather than sampling for this purpose because the survey is not immediately able to bring new businesses into the sample. There is an unavoidable lag between the birth of a new firm and its appearance on the sampling frame and availability for selection. BLS adds new businesses to the survey twice a year.

6. Is the count of unemployed persons limited to just those people receiving unemployment insurance benefits?

No; the estimate of unemployment is based on a monthly sample survey of households. All persons who are without jobs and are actively seeking and available to work are included among the unemployed. (People on temporary layoff are included even if they do not actively seek work.) There is no requirement or question relating to unemployment insurance benefits in the monthly survey.

7. Does the official unemployment rate exclude people who want a job but are not currently looking for work?

Yes; however, there are separate estimates of persons outside the labor force who want a job, including those who are not currently looking because they believe no jobs are available (discouraged workers). In addition, alternative measures of labor underutilization (some of which include discouraged workers and other groups not officially counted as unemployed) are published each month in table A-15 of The Employment Situation news release. For more information about these alternative measures, please visit www.bls.gov/cps/lfcharacteristics.htm#altmeasures.

8. How can unusually severe weather affect employment and hours estimates?

In the establishment survey, the reference period is the pay period that includes the 12th of the month. Unusually severe weather is more likely to have an impact on average weekly hours than on employment. Average weekly hours are estimated for paid time during the pay period, including pay for holidays, sick leave, or other time off. The impact of severe weather on hours estimates typically, but not always, results in a reduction in average weekly hours. For example, some employees may be off work for part of the pay period and not receive pay for the time missed, while some workers, such as those dealing with cleanup or repair, may work extra hours.

Typically, it is not possible to precisely quantify the effect of extreme weather on payroll employment estimates. In order for severe weather conditions to reduce employment estimates, employees have to be off work without pay for the entire pay period. Employees who receive pay for any part of the pay period, even 1 hour, are counted in the payroll employment figures. For more information on how often employees are paid, please visit www.bls.gov/opub/btn/volume-3/how-frequently-do-private-businesses-pay-workers.htm.

In the household survey, the reference period is generally the calendar week that includes the 12th of the month. Persons who miss the entire week's work for weather-related events are counted as employed whether or not they are paid for the time off. The household survey collects data on the number of persons who had a job but were not at work due to bad weather. It also provides a measure of the number of persons who usually work full time but had reduced hours due to bad weather. Current and historical data are available on the household survey's most requested statistics page, please visit http://data.bls.gov/cgi-bin/surveymost?ln.

Technical Note

This news release presents statistics from two major surveys, the Current Population Survey (CPS; household survey) and the Current Employment Statistics survey (CES; establishment survey). The household survey provides information on the labor force, employment, and unemployment that appears in the "A" tables, marked HOUSEHOLD DATA. It is a sample survey of about 60,000 eligible households conducted by the U.S. Census Bureau for the U.S. Bureau of Labor Statistics (BLS).

The establishment survey provides information on employment, hours, and earnings of employees on nonfarm payrolls; the data appear in the "B" tables, marked ESTABLISHMENT DATA. BLS collects these data each month from the payroll records of a sample of nonagricultural business establishments. Each month the CES program surveys about 143,000 businesses and government agencies, representing approximately 588,000 individual worksites, in order to provide detailed industry data on employment, hours, and earnings of workers on nonfarm payrolls. The active sample includes approximately one-third of all nonfarm payroll employees.

For both surveys, the data for a given month relate to a particular week or pay period. In the household survey, the reference period is generally the calendar week that contains the 12th day of the month. In the establishment survey, the reference period is the pay period including the 12th, which may or may not correspond directly to the calendar week.

Coverage, definitions, and differences between surveys

Household survey. The sample is selected to reflect the entire civilian noninstitutional population. Based on responses to a series of questions on work and job search activities, each person 16 years and over in a sample household is classified as employed, unemployed, or not in the labor force.

People are classified as *employed* if they did any work at all as paid employees during the reference week; worked in their own business, profession, or on their own farm; or worked without pay at least 15 hours in a family business or farm. People are also counted as employed if they were temporarily absent from their jobs because of illness, bad weather, vacation, labor-management disputes, or personal reasons.

People are classified as *unemployed* if they meet all of the following criteria: they had no employment during the reference week; they were available for work at that time; and they made specific efforts to find employment sometime during the 4-week period ending with the reference week. Persons laid off from a job and expecting recall need not be looking for work to be counted as unemployed. The unemployment data derived from the household survey in no way depend upon the eligibility for or receipt of unemployment insurance benefits.

The *civilian labor force* is the sum of employed and unemployed persons. Those persons not classified as employed or unemployed are *not in the labor force*. The *unemployment rate* is the number unemployed as a percent of the labor force. The *labor force participation rate* is the labor force as a percent of the population, and the *employment-population ratio* is the employed as a percent of the population. Additional information about the household survey can be found at www.bls.gov/cps/documentation.htm.

Establishment survey. The sample establishments are drawn from private nonfarm businesses such as factories, offices, and stores, as well as from federal, state, and local government entities. *Employees on nonfarm payrolls* are those who received pay for any part of the reference pay period, including persons on paid leave. Persons are counted in each job they hold. *Hours and earnings* data are produced for the private sector for all employees and for production and nonsupervisory employees. *Production and nonsupervisory* employees are defined as production and related employees in manufacturing and mining and logging, construction workers in construction, and non-supervisory employees in private service-providing industries.

Industries are classified on the basis of an establishment's principal activity in accordance with the 2012 version of the North American Industry Classification System. Additional information about the establishment survey can be found at www.bls.gov/ces/.

Differences in employment estimates. The numerous conceptual and methodological differences between the household and establishment surveys result in important distinctions in the employment estimates derived from the surveys. Among these are:

- The household survey includes agricultural workers, self-employed workers whose businesses are unincorporated, unpaid family workers, and private household workers among the employed. These groups are excluded from the establishment survey.

- The household survey includes people on unpaid leave among the employed. The establishment survey does not.

- The household survey is limited to workers 16 years of age and older. The establishment survey is not limited by age.

- The household survey has no duplication of individuals, because individuals are counted only once, even if they hold more than one job. In the establishment survey, employees working at more than one job and thus appearing on more than one payroll are counted separately for each appearance.

Seasonal adjustment

Over the course of a year, the size of the nation's labor force and the levels of employment and unemployment undergo regularly occurring fluctuations. These events may result from seasonal changes in weather, major holidays, and the opening and closing of schools. The effect of such seasonal variation can be very large.

Because these seasonal events follow a more or less regular pattern each year, their influence on the level of a series can be tempered by adjusting for regular seasonal variation. These adjustments make nonseasonal developments, such as declines in employment or increases in the participation of women in the labor force, easier to spot. For example, in the household survey, the large number of youth entering the labor force each June is likely to obscure any other changes that have taken place relative to May, making it difficult to determine if the level of economic activity has risen or declined. Similarly, in the establishment survey, payroll employment in education declines by about 20 percent at the end of the spring term and later rises with the start of the fall term, obscuring the underlying employment trends in the industry. Because seasonal employment changes at the end and beginning of the school year can be estimated, the statistics can be adjusted to make underlying employment patterns more discernable. The seasonally adjusted figures provide a more useful tool with which to analyze changes in month-to-month economic activity.

Many seasonally adjusted series are independently adjusted in both the household and establishment surveys. However, the adjusted series for many major estimates, such as total payroll employment, employment in most major sectors, total employment, and unemployment are computed by aggregating independently adjusted component series. For example, total unemployment is derived by summing the adjusted series for four major age-sex components; this differs from the unemployment estimate that would be obtained by directly adjusting the total or by combining the duration, reasons, or more detailed age categories.

For both the household and establishment surveys, a concurrent seasonal adjustment methodology is used in which new seasonal factors are calculated each month using all relevant data, up to and including the data for the current month. In the household survey, new seasonal factors are used to adjust only the current month's data. In the establishment survey, however, new seasonal factors are used each month to adjust the three most recent monthly estimates. The prior 2 months are routinely revised to incorporate additional sample reports and recalculated seasonal adjustment factors. In both surveys, 5-year revisions to historical data are made once a year.

Reliability of the estimates

Statistics based on the household and establishment surveys are subject to both sampling and nonsampling error. When a sample, rather than the entire population, is surveyed, there is a chance that the sample estimates may differ from the true population values they represent. The component of this difference that occurs because samples differ by chance is known as *sampling error*, and its variability is measured by the standard error of the estimate. There is about a 90-percent chance, or level of confidence, that an estimate based on a sample will differ by no more than 1.6 standard errors from the true population value because of sampling error. BLS analyses are generally conducted at the 90-percent level of confidence.

For example, the confidence interval for the monthly change in total nonfarm employment from the establishment survey is on the order of plus or minus 105,000. Suppose the estimate of nonfarm employment increases by 50,000 from one month to the next. The 90-percent confidence interval on the monthly change would range from -55,000 to +155,000 (50,000 +/- 105,000). These figures do not mean that the sample results are off by these magnitudes, but rather that there is about a 90-percent chance that the true over-the-month change lies within this interval. Since this range includes values of less than zero, we could not say with confidence that nonfarm employment had, in fact, increased that month. If, however, the reported nonfarm employment rise was 250,000, then all of the values within the 90-percent confidence interval would be greater than zero. In this case, it is likely (at least a 90-percent chance) that nonfarm employment had, in fact, risen that month. At an unemployment rate of around 6.0 percent, the 90-percent confidence interval for the monthly change in unemployment as measured by the household survey is about +/- 300,000, and for the monthly change in the unemployment rate it is about +/- 0.2 percentage point.

In general, estimates involving many individuals or establishments have lower standard errors (relative to the size of the estimate) than estimates which are based on a small number of observations. The precision of estimates also is improved when the data are cumulated over time, such as for quarterly and annual averages.

The household and establishment surveys are also affected by *nonsampling error*, which can occur for many reasons, including the failure to sample a segment of the population, inability to obtain information for all respondents in the sample, inability or unwillingness of respondents to provide correct information on a timely basis, mistakes made by respondents, and errors made in the collection or processing of the data.

For example, in the establishment survey, estimates for the most recent 2 months are based on incomplete returns; for this reason, these estimates are labeled preliminary in the tables. It is only after two successive revisions to a monthly estimate, when nearly all sample reports have been received, that the estimate is considered final.

Another major source of nonsampling error in the establishment survey is the inability to capture, on a timely basis, employment generated by new firms. To correct for this systematic underestimation of employment growth, an estimation procedure with two components is used to account for business births. The first component excludes employment losses from business deaths from sample-based estimation in order to offset the missing employment gains from business births. This is incorporated into the sample-based estimation procedure by simply not reflecting sample units going out of business, but imputing to them the same employment trend as the other firms in the sample. This procedure accounts for most of the net birth/death employment.

The second component is an ARIMA time series model designed to estimate the residual net birth/death employment not accounted for by the imputation. The historical time series used to create and test the ARIMA model was derived from the unemployment insurance universe micro-level database, and reflects the actual residual net of births and deaths over the past 5 years.

The sample-based estimates from the establishment survey are adjusted once a year (on a lagged basis) to universe counts of payroll employment obtained from administrative records of the unemployment insurance program. The difference between the March sample-based employment estimates and the March universe counts is known as a benchmark revision, and serves as a rough proxy for total survey error. The new benchmarks also incorporate changes in the classification of industries. Over the past decade, absolute benchmark revisions for total nonfarm employment have averaged 0.3 percent, with a range from -0.7 to 0.6 percent.

Other information

Information in this release will be made available to sensory impaired individuals upon request. Voice phone: (202) 691-5200; Federal Relay Service: (800) 877-8339.

HOUSEHOLD DATA
Table A-1. Employment status of the civilian population by sex and age
[Numbers in thousands]

Employment status, sex, and age	Not seasonally adjusted			Seasonally adjusted[1]					
	Feb. 2014	Jan. 2015	Feb. 2015	Feb. 2014	Oct. 2014	Nov. 2014	Dec. 2014	Jan. 2015	Feb. 2015
TOTAL									
Civilian noninstitutional population	247,085	249,723	249,899	247,085	248,657	248,844	249,027	249,723	249,899
Civilian labor force	155,027	156,050	156,213	155,688	156,243	156,402	156,129	157,180	157,002
Participation rate	62.7	62.5	62.5	63.0	62.8	62.9	62.7	62.9	62.8
Employed	144,134	146,552	147,118	145,301	147,260	147,331	147,442	148,201	148,297
Employment-population ratio	58.3	58.7	58.9	58.8	59.2	59.2	59.2	59.3	59.3
Unemployed	10,893	9,498	9,095	10,387	8,983	9,071	8,688	8,979	8,705
Unemployment rate	7.0	6.1	5.8	6.7	5.7	5.8	5.6	5.7	5.5
Not in labor force	92,058	93,674	93,686	91,398	92,414	92,442	92,898	92,544	92,898
Persons who currently want a job	6,091	6,467	6,575	6,072	6,545	6,556	6,445	6,358	6,538
Men, 16 years and over									
Civilian noninstitutional population	119,306	120,559	120,647	119,306	120,112	120,208	120,301	120,559	120,647
Civilian labor force	81,954	82,851	83,040	82,566	82,950	82,961	83,210	83,771	83,772
Participation rate	68.7	68.7	68.8	69.2	69.1	69.0	69.2	69.5	69.4
Employed	75,687	77,477	77,824	76,852	78,286	78,084	78,400	78,869	79,006
Employment-population ratio	63.4	64.3	64.5	64.4	65.2	65.0	65.2	65.4	65.5
Unemployed	6,267	5,374	5,216	5,714	4,664	4,877	4,810	4,903	4,766
Unemployment rate	7.6	6.5	6.3	6.9	5.6	5.9	5.8	5.9	5.7
Not in labor force	37,352	37,708	37,607	36,740	37,161	37,247	37,091	36,787	36,875
Men, 20 years and over									
Civilian noninstitutional population	110,838	112,117	112,209	110,838	111,679	111,778	111,875	112,117	112,209
Civilian labor force	79,528	80,179	80,394	79,884	80,023	80,029	80,271	80,804	80,831
Participation rate	71.8	71.5	71.6	72.1	71.7	71.6	71.8	72.1	72.0
Employed	73,882	75,364	75,671	74,820	75,928	75,675	76,026	76,496	76,588
Employment-population ratio	66.7	67.2	67.4	67.5	68.0	67.7	68.0	68.2	68.3
Unemployed	5,645	4,815	4,723	5,064	4,094	4,354	4,245	4,308	4,243
Unemployment rate	7.1	6.0	5.9	6.3	5.1	5.4	5.3	5.3	5.2
Not in labor force	31,310	31,938	31,816	30,954	31,656	31,749	31,603	31,313	31,379
Women, 16 years and over									
Civilian noninstitutional population	127,779	129,165	129,252	127,779	128,545	128,637	128,726	129,165	129,252
Civilian labor force	73,073	73,199	73,173	73,122	73,293	73,442	72,919	73,408	73,230
Participation rate	57.2	56.7	56.6	57.2	57.0	57.1	56.6	56.8	56.7
Employed	68,446	69,075	69,294	68,449	68,974	69,247	69,042	69,332	69,291
Employment-population ratio	53.6	53.5	53.6	53.6	53.7	53.8	53.6	53.7	53.6
Unemployed	4,626	4,124	3,879	4,673	4,318	4,195	3,878	4,076	3,939
Unemployment rate	6.3	5.6	5.3	6.4	5.9	5.7	5.3	5.6	5.4
Not in labor force	54,707	55,966	56,079	54,657	55,253	55,195	55,807	55,756	56,023
Women, 20 years and over									
Civilian noninstitutional population	119,583	120,970	121,060	119,583	120,370	120,465	120,557	120,970	121,060
Civilian labor force	70,493	70,554	70,526	70,323	70,354	70,599	70,111	70,558	70,370
Participation rate	58.9	58.3	58.3	58.8	58.4	58.6	58.2	58.3	58.1
Employed	66,319	66,894	67,058	66,168	66,560	66,894	66,632	66,983	66,901
Employment-population ratio	55.5	55.3	55.4	55.3	55.3	55.5	55.3	55.4	55.3
Unemployed	4,175	3,660	3,468	4,155	3,794	3,705	3,479	3,575	3,469
Unemployment rate	5.9	5.2	4.9	5.9	5.4	5.2	5.0	5.1	4.9
Not in labor force	49,089	50,416	50,534	49,260	50,016	49,866	50,446	50,412	50,690
Both sexes, 16 to 19 years									
Civilian noninstitutional population	16,664	16,636	16,630	16,664	16,608	16,602	16,595	16,636	16,630
Civilian labor force	5,006	5,317	5,293	5,480	5,866	5,775	5,747	5,817	5,801
Participation rate	30.0	32.0	31.8	32.9	35.3	34.8	34.6	35.0	34.9
Employed	3,933	4,294	4,389	4,312	4,772	4,762	4,784	4,722	4,808
Employment-population ratio	23.6	25.8	26.4	25.9	28.7	28.7	28.8	28.4	28.9
Unemployed	1,073	1,023	904	1,168	1,094	1,013	963	1,096	993
Unemployment rate	21.4	19.2	17.1	21.3	18.7	17.5	16.8	18.8	17.1
Not in labor force	11,658	11,320	11,337	11,184	10,742	10,827	10,849	10,819	10,829

[1] The population figures are not adjusted for seasonal variation; therefore, identical numbers appear in the unadjusted and seasonally adjusted columns.
NOTE: Updated population controls are introduced annually with the release of January data.

Table A-2. Employment status of the civilian population by race, sex, and age

[Numbers in thousands]

Employment status, race, sex, and age	Not seasonally adjusted			Seasonally adjusted[1]					
	Feb. 2014	Jan. 2015	Feb. 2015	Feb. 2014	Oct. 2014	Nov. 2014	Dec. 2014	Jan. 2015	Feb. 2015
WHITE									
Civilian noninstitutional population	195,029	196,307	196,392	195,029	195,896	195,995	196,091	196,307	196,392
Civilian labor force	122,928	123,199	123,224	123,554	123,287	123,391	123,058	124,119	123,875
Participation rate	63.0	62.8	62.7	63.4	62.9	63.0	62.8	63.2	63.1
Employed	115,312	116,637	116,944	116,425	117,300	117,307	117,186	118,035	117,992
Employment-population ratio	59.1	59.4	59.5	59.7	59.9	59.9	59.8	60.1	60.1
Unemployed	7,616	6,562	6,279	7,130	5,987	6,084	5,872	6,084	5,883
Unemployment rate	6.2	5.3	5.1	5.8	4.9	4.9	4.8	4.9	4.7
Not in labor force	72,101	73,109	73,169	71,474	72,609	72,604	73,033	72,189	72,517
Men, 20 years and over									
Civilian labor force	64,185	64,377	64,559	64,531	64,234	64,339	64,392	64,871	64,920
Participation rate	72.2	71.9	72.0	72.6	71.8	71.9	71.9	72.4	72.4
Employed	60,178	61,016	61,228	61,013	61,507	61,388	61,551	61,953	62,015
Employment-population ratio	67.7	68.1	68.3	68.6	68.8	68.6	68.8	69.2	69.2
Unemployed	4,008	3,361	3,330	3,518	2,727	2,951	2,842	2,918	2,906
Unemployment rate	6.2	5.2	5.2	5.5	4.2	4.6	4.4	4.5	4.5
Women, 20 years and over									
Civilian labor force	54,709	54,635	54,499	54,615	54,452	54,587	54,223	54,683	54,401
Participation rate	58.4	57.9	57.7	58.3	57.9	58.0	57.5	57.9	57.6
Employed	51,866	52,140	52,186	51,815	51,945	52,142	51,824	52,267	52,105
Employment-population ratio	55.4	55.2	55.3	55.3	55.2	55.4	55.0	55.4	55.2
Unemployed	2,843	2,495	2,312	2,800	2,507	2,445	2,399	2,416	2,296
Unemployment rate	5.2	4.6	4.2	5.1	4.6	4.5	4.4	4.4	4.2
Both sexes, 16 to 19 years									
Civilian labor force	4,033	4,186	4,166	4,408	4,601	4,466	4,443	4,565	4,554
Participation rate	32.5	33.9	33.8	35.5	37.2	36.2	36.0	37.0	36.9
Employed	3,268	3,481	3,529	3,596	3,848	3,777	3,811	3,814	3,872
Employment-population ratio	26.3	28.2	28.6	29.0	31.1	30.6	30.9	30.9	31.4
Unemployed	765	706	637	812	753	689	632	751	682
Unemployment rate	19.0	16.9	15.3	18.4	16.4	15.4	14.2	16.4	15.0
BLACK OR AFRICAN AMERICAN									
Civilian noninstitutional population	30,685	31,188	31,222	30,685	30,969	31,005	31,040	31,188	31,222
Civilian labor force	18,591	18,895	18,941	18,723	19,024	19,056	19,037	19,040	19,101
Participation rate	60.6	60.6	60.7	61.0	61.4	61.5	61.3	61.0	61.2
Employed	16,351	16,877	16,975	16,486	16,953	16,957	17,050	17,071	17,122
Employment-population ratio	53.3	54.1	54.4	53.7	54.7	54.7	54.9	54.7	54.8
Unemployed	2,240	2,018	1,966	2,238	2,071	2,099	1,986	1,969	1,979
Unemployment rate	12.0	10.7	10.4	12.0	10.9	11.0	10.4	10.3	10.4
Not in labor force	12,094	12,293	12,281	11,962	11,945	11,949	12,003	12,148	12,122
Men, 20 years and over									
Civilian labor force	8,417	8,633	8,628	8,485	8,672	8,594	8,717	8,676	8,710
Participation rate	66.5	66.8	66.6	67.0	67.6	66.9	67.8	67.1	67.3
Employed	7,279	7,652	7,685	7,398	7,742	7,630	7,756	7,757	7,805
Employment-population ratio	57.5	59.2	59.4	58.4	60.4	59.4	60.3	60.0	60.3
Unemployed	1,138	981	943	1,087	930	964	962	919	905
Unemployment rate	13.5	11.4	10.9	12.8	10.7	11.2	11.0	10.6	10.4
Women, 20 years and over									
Civilian labor force	9,611	9,638	9,656	9,616	9,624	9,709	9,598	9,667	9,665
Participation rate	62.0	61.2	61.2	62.0	61.5	61.9	61.2	61.3	61.3
Employed	8,687	8,792	8,820	8,669	8,720	8,786	8,812	8,824	8,809
Employment-population ratio	56.0	55.8	55.9	55.9	55.7	56.1	56.2	56.0	55.8
Unemployed	925	847	835	947	904	922	785	843	857
Unemployment rate	9.6	8.8	8.7	9.8	9.4	9.5	8.2	8.7	8.9
Both sexes, 16 to 19 years									
Civilian labor force	562	624	658	622	728	754	722	697	726
Participation rate	22.3	24.9	26.4	24.7	29.2	30.2	29.0	27.9	29.1
Employed	385	433	471	418	491	541	482	490	508
Employment-population ratio	15.3	17.3	18.8	16.6	19.7	21.7	19.4	19.6	20.4
Unemployed	177	191	188	204	237	213	240	207	218
Unemployment rate	31.5	30.6	28.5	32.8	32.5	28.2	33.2	29.7	30.0
ASIAN									
Civilian noninstitutional population	13,738	14,253	14,291	13,738	13,782	13,927	13,886	14,253	14,291

See footnotes at end of table.

Table A-2. Employment status of the civilian population by race, sex, and age — Continued

[Numbers in thousands]

Employment status, race, sex, and age	Not seasonally adjusted			Seasonally adjusted[1]					
	Feb. 2014	Jan. 2015	Feb. 2015	Feb. 2014	Oct. 2014	Nov. 2014	Dec. 2014	Jan. 2015	Feb. 2015
Civilian labor force....................................	8,797	8,895	9,042	8,805	8,782	8,768	8,771	8,899	9,038
Participation rate.................................	64.0	62.4	63.3	64.1	63.7	63.0	63.2	62.4	63.2
Employed...	8,270	8,530	8,672	8,289	8,340	8,353	8,398	8,540	8,680
Employment-population ratio....................	60.2	59.8	60.7	60.3	60.5	60.0	60.5	59.9	60.7
Unemployed.......................................	528	365	369	515	443	415	373	359	358
Unemployment rate.............................	6.0	4.1	4.1	5.9	5.0	4.7	4.2	4.0	4.0
Not in labor force....................................	4,941	5,359	5,249	4,934	5,000	5,159	5,115	5,355	5,253

[1] The population figures are not adjusted for seasonal variation; therefore, identical numbers appear in the unadjusted and seasonally adjusted columns.

NOTE: Estimates for the above race groups will not sum to totals shown in table A-1 because data are not presented for all races. Updated population controls are introduced annually with the release of January data.

Table A-3. Employment status of the Hispanic or Latino population by sex and age
[Numbers in thousands]

Employment status, sex, and age	Not seasonally adjusted			Seasonally adjusted[1]					
	Feb. 2014	Jan. 2015	Feb. 2015	Feb. 2014	Oct. 2014	Nov. 2014	Dec. 2014	Jan. 2015	Feb. 2015
HISPANIC OR LATINO ETHNICITY									
Civilian noninstitutional population................	38,053	39,165	39,244	38,053	38,679	38,760	38,839	39,165	39,244
Civilian labor force..............................	25,019	25,956	25,850	25,155	25,665	25,655	25,644	26,047	25,962
Participation rate.............................	65.7	66.3	65.9	66.1	66.4	66.2	66.0	66.5	66.2
Employed......................................	22,836	23,998	23,975	23,112	23,931	23,963	23,988	24,305	24,238
Employment-population ratio..............	60.0	61.3	61.1	60.7	61.9	61.8	61.8	62.1	61.8
Unemployed...................................	2,183	1,958	1,875	2,043	1,734	1,692	1,656	1,742	1,724
Unemployment rate.........................	8.7	7.5	7.3	8.1	6.8	6.6	6.5	6.7	6.6
Not in labor force..............................	13,033	13,208	13,395	12,897	13,013	13,105	13,196	13,118	13,282
Men, 20 years and over									
Civilian labor force..............................	13,821	14,426	14,388	13,918	14,218	14,258	14,264	14,479	14,465
Participation rate.............................	80.4	81.8	81.4	80.9	81.2	81.3	81.1	82.1	81.8
Employed......................................	12,806	13,413	13,397	13,011	13,458	13,432	13,507	13,647	13,601
Employment-population ratio..............	74.5	76.0	75.8	75.6	76.9	76.5	76.8	77.3	76.9
Unemployed...................................	1,015	1,013	991	907	760	826	757	832	864
Unemployment rate.........................	7.3	7.0	6.9	6.5	5.3	5.8	5.3	5.7	6.0
Women, 20 years and over									
Civilian labor force..............................	10,196	10,364	10,333	10,177	10,259	10,253	10,168	10,344	10,309
Participation rate.............................	59.3	58.1	57.8	59.2	58.6	58.5	57.9	58.0	57.7
Employed......................................	9,301	9,677	9,667	9,331	9,522	9,590	9,501	9,704	9,685
Employment-population ratio..............	54.1	54.3	54.1	54.2	54.4	54.7	54.1	54.4	54.2
Unemployed...................................	895	687	666	846	737	663	667	640	625
Unemployment rate.........................	8.8	6.6	6.4	8.3	7.2	6.5	6.6	6.2	6.1
Both sexes, 16 to 19 years									
Civilian labor force..............................	1,002	1,165	1,129	1,060	1,187	1,144	1,211	1,224	1,187
Participation rate.............................	27.5	31.6	30.6	29.1	32.3	31.1	32.9	33.2	32.2
Employed......................................	729	908	911	770	950	942	980	954	952
Employment-population ratio..............	20.0	24.6	24.7	21.1	25.9	25.6	26.6	25.9	25.8
Unemployed...................................	274	257	218	290	237	202	231	270	235
Unemployment rate.........................	27.3	22.1	19.3	27.4	20.0	17.7	19.1	22.1	19.8

[1] The population figures are not adjusted for seasonal variation; therefore, identical numbers appear in the unadjusted and seasonally adjusted columns.

NOTE: Persons whose ethnicity is identified as Hispanic or Latino may be of any race. Updated population controls are introduced annually with the release of January data.

HOUSEHOLD DATA

Table A-4. Employment status of the civilian population 25 years and over by educational attainment

[Numbers in thousands]

Educational attainment	Not seasonally adjusted			Seasonally adjusted					
	Feb. 2014	Jan. 2015	Feb. 2015	Feb. 2014	Oct. 2014	Nov. 2014	Dec. 2014	Jan. 2015	Feb. 2015
Less than a high school diploma									
Civilian labor force..................................	10,804	11,353	10,867	11,078	10,831	11,153	11,031	11,439	11,126
Participation rate...................................	44.8	45.7	45.2	45.9	45.3	45.7	45.4	46.0	46.3
Employed...	9,602	10,226	9,842	9,993	9,975	10,201	10,079	10,468	10,196
Employment-population ratio................	39.8	41.1	41.0	41.4	41.7	41.8	41.5	42.1	42.4
Unemployed.......................................	1,203	1,126	1,025	1,084	856	952	952	971	929
Unemployment rate............................	11.1	9.9	9.4	9.8	7.9	8.5	8.6	8.5	8.4
High school graduates, no college[1]									
Civilian labor force..................................	36,050	35,238	35,142	36,227	36,183	35,478	35,164	35,418	35,371
Participation rate...................................	58.4	57.6	57.0	58.6	58.0	57.8	57.5	57.9	57.4
Employed...	33,482	33,083	33,037	33,903	34,127	33,476	33,310	33,492	33,464
Employment-population ratio................	54.2	54.1	53.6	54.9	54.7	54.5	54.5	54.8	54.3
Unemployed.......................................	2,568	2,155	2,106	2,324	2,056	2,002	1,854	1,926	1,907
Unemployment rate............................	7.1	6.1	6.0	6.4	5.7	5.6	5.3	5.4	5.4
Some college or associate degree									
Civilian labor force..................................	37,261	37,208	37,457	37,255	37,304	37,246	37,140	37,479	37,490
Participation rate...................................	67.1	66.7	66.7	67.0	66.5	66.7	66.9	67.2	66.8
Employed...	34,898	35,118	35,441	35,006	35,460	35,422	35,310	35,540	35,588
Employment-population ratio................	62.8	63.0	63.1	63.0	63.2	63.5	63.6	63.8	63.4
Unemployed.......................................	2,363	2,090	2,015	2,249	1,843	1,824	1,831	1,939	1,902
Unemployment rate............................	6.3	5.6	5.4	6.0	4.9	4.9	4.9	5.2	5.1
Bachelor's degree and higher[2]									
Civilian labor force..................................	50,522	51,695	51,996	50,169	50,471	51,222	51,772	51,550	51,583
Participation rate...................................	75.6	74.7	74.9	75.1	74.6	74.7	74.6	74.4	74.4
Employed...	48,796	50,212	50,576	48,468	48,937	49,608	50,290	50,084	50,172
Employment-population ratio................	73.0	72.5	72.9	72.5	72.4	72.3	72.5	72.3	72.3
Unemployed.......................................	1,726	1,483	1,421	1,700	1,534	1,614	1,482	1,466	1,411
Unemployment rate............................	3.4	2.9	2.7	3.4	3.0	3.2	2.9	2.8	2.7

[1] Includes persons with a high school diploma or equivalent.

[2] Includes persons with bachelor's, master's, professional, and doctoral degrees.

NOTE: Updated population controls are introduced annually with the release of January data.

Table A-5. Employment status of the civilian population 18 years and over by veteran status, period of service, and sex, not seasonally adjusted

[Numbers in thousands]

Employment status, veteran status, and period of service	Total		Men		Women	
	Feb. 2014	Feb. 2015	Feb. 2014	Feb. 2015	Feb. 2014	Feb. 2015
VETERANS, 18 years and over						
Civilian noninstitutional population.	21,298	21,326	19,054	19,335	2,244	1,991
Civilian labor force.	10,833	10,903	9,389	9,577	1,445	1,326
Participation rate.	50.9	51.1	49.3	49.5	64.4	66.6
Employed.	10,149	10,325	8,781	9,076	1,368	1,250
Employment-population ratio.	47.7	48.4	46.1	46.9	61.0	62.8
Unemployed.	684	578	608	502	76	76
Unemployment rate.	6.3	5.3	6.5	5.2	5.3	5.7
Not in labor force.	10,465	10,423	9,665	9,758	799	665
Gulf War-era II veterans						
Civilian noninstitutional population.	2,995	3,421	2,415	2,838	581	584
Civilian labor force.	2,430	2,825	2,020	2,404	410	421
Participation rate.	81.1	82.6	83.7	84.7	70.6	72.2
Employed.	2,207	2,635	1,838	2,230	370	405
Employment-population ratio.	73.7	77.0	76.1	78.6	63.7	69.3
Unemployed.	223	190	183	174	40	17
Unemployment rate.	9.2	6.7	9.0	7.2	9.9	4.0
Not in labor force.	565	596	394	434	171	163
Gulf War-era I veterans						
Civilian noninstitutional population.	3,412	3,533	2,707	2,965	704	567
Civilian labor force.	2,787	2,885	2,284	2,450	503	435
Participation rate.	81.7	81.7	84.3	82.6	71.4	76.6
Employed.	2,658	2,777	2,177	2,378	481	400
Employment-population ratio.	77.9	78.6	80.4	80.2	68.3	70.5
Unemployed.	128	107	107	72	22	35
Unemployment rate.	4.6	3.7	4.7	2.9	4.3	8.1
Not in labor force.	625	648	424	515	201	132
World War II, Korean War, and Vietnam-era veterans						
Civilian noninstitutional population.	9,554	9,057	9,195	8,735	359	322
Civilian labor force.	2,817	2,419	2,718	2,293	99	127
Participation rate.	29.5	26.7	29.6	26.2	27.6	39.4
Employed.	2,633	2,293	2,539	2,177	95	116
Employment-population ratio.	27.6	25.3	27.6	24.9	26.4	36.0
Unemployed.	184	126	179	115	4	11
Unemployment rate.	6.5	5.2	6.6	5.0	4.4	8.5
Not in labor force.	6,737	6,638	6,477	6,442	260	195
Veterans of other service periods						
Civilian noninstitutional population.	5,337	5,315	4,737	4,797	600	518
Civilian labor force.	2,799	2,774	2,367	2,431	432	343
Participation rate.	52.4	52.2	50.0	50.7	72.0	66.2
Employed.	2,650	2,620	2,227	2,290	422	330
Employment-population ratio.	49.6	49.3	47.0	47.7	70.4	63.7
Unemployed.	149	154	140	141	10	13
Unemployment rate.	5.3	5.6	5.9	5.8	2.2	3.9
Not in labor force.	2,538	2,541	2,370	2,366	168	175
NONVETERANS, 18 years and over						
Civilian noninstitutional population.	216,827	219,793	95,685	96,888	121,142	122,906
Civilian labor force.	142,531	143,572	71,799	72,636	70,732	70,936
Participation rate.	65.7	65.3	75.0	75.0	58.4	57.7
Employed.	132,676	135,360	66,338	68,082	66,338	67,278
Employment-population ratio.	61.2	61.6	69.3	70.3	54.8	54.7
Unemployed.	9,854	8,212	5,460	4,554	4,394	3,658
Unemployment rate.	6.9	5.7	7.6	6.3	6.2	5.2
Not in labor force.	74,296	76,222	23,887	24,252	50,410	51,970

NOTE: Veterans served on active duty in the U.S. Armed Forces and were not on active duty at the time of the survey. Nonveterans never served on active duty in the U.S. Armed Forces. Veterans could have served anywhere in the world during these periods of service: Gulf War era II (September 2001-present), Gulf War era I (August 1990-August 2001), Vietnam era (August 1964-April 1975), Korean War (July 1950-January 1955), World War II (December 1941-December 1946), and other service periods (all other time periods). Veterans who served in more than one wartime period are classified only in the most recent one. Veterans who served during one of the selected wartime periods and another period are classified only in the wartime period.

Table A-6. Employment status of the civilian population by sex, age, and disability status, not seasonally adjusted

[Numbers in thousands]

Employment status, sex, and age	Persons with a disability		Persons with no disability	
	Feb. 2014	Feb. 2015	Feb. 2014	Feb. 2015
TOTAL, 16 years and over				
Civilian noninstitutional population..	28,970	29,316	218,116	220,584
Civilian labor force..	5,537	5,806	149,490	150,407
Participation rate..	19.1	19.8	68.5	68.2
Employed...	4,746	5,153	139,388	141,965
Employment-population ratio...	16.4	17.6	63.9	64.4
Unemployed..	792	653	10,102	8,442
Unemployment rate..	14.3	11.2	6.8	5.6
Not in labor force...	23,433	23,510	68,626	70,177
Men, 16 to 64 years				
Civilian labor force..	2,454	2,637	74,918	75,718
Participation rate..	32.2	34.3	81.4	81.8
Employed...	2,042	2,321	69,248	71,047
Employment-population ratio...	26.8	30.1	75.3	76.8
Unemployed..	412	316	5,670	4,671
Unemployment rate..	16.8	12.0	7.6	6.2
Not in labor force...	5,173	5,061	17,082	16,820
Women, 16 to 64 years				
Civilian labor force..	2,097	2,201	67,167	66,993
Participation rate..	26.8	28.0	70.5	69.9
Employed...	1,762	1,925	63,048	63,564
Employment-population ratio...	22.6	24.5	66.2	66.3
Unemployed..	334	276	4,119	3,429
Unemployment rate..	15.9	12.5	6.1	5.1
Not in labor force...	5,719	5,647	28,074	28,886
Both sexes, 65 years and over				
Civilian labor force..	986	967	7,405	7,696
Participation rate..	7.3	7.0	24.0	23.9
Employed...	941	907	7,092	7,354
Employment-population ratio...	7.0	6.6	23.0	22.9
Unemployed..	45	60	313	342
Unemployment rate..	4.6	6.2	4.2	4.4
Not in labor force...	12,541	12,802	23,470	24,471

NOTE: A person with a disability has at least one of the following conditions: is deaf or has serious difficulty hearing; is blind or has serious difficulty seeing even when wearing glasses; has serious difficulty concentrating, remembering, or making decisions because of a physical, mental, or emotional condition; has serious difficulty walking or climbing stairs; has difficulty dressing or bathing; or has difficulty doing errands alone such as visiting a doctor's office or shopping because of a physical, mental, or emotional condition. Updated population controls are introduced annually with the release of January data.

Table A-7. Employment status of the civilian population by nativity and sex, not seasonally adjusted

[Numbers in thousands]

Employment status and nativity	Total		Men		Women	
	Feb. 2014	Feb. 2015	Feb. 2014	Feb. 2015	Feb. 2014	Feb. 2015
Foreign born, 16 years and over						
Civilian noninstitutional population...................................	38,188	40,300	18,429	19,540	19,759	20,760
Civilian labor force..	25,421	26,276	14,612	15,233	10,809	11,043
Participation rate..	66.6	65.2	79.3	78.0	54.7	53.2
Employed..	23,658	24,741	13,693	14,326	9,964	10,414
Employment-population ratio.................................	61.9	61.4	74.3	73.3	50.4	50.2
Unemployed..	1,763	1,536	919	907	845	629
Unemployment rate...	6.9	5.8	6.3	6.0	7.8	5.7
Not in labor force...	12,768	14,023	3,817	4,306	8,951	9,717
Native born, 16 years and over						
Civilian noninstitutional population...................................	208,897	209,600	100,877	101,108	108,020	108,492
Civilian labor force..	129,606	129,937	67,342	67,807	62,264	62,130
Participation rate..	62.0	62.0	66.8	67.1	57.6	57.3
Employed..	120,476	122,378	61,994	63,497	58,482	58,880
Employment-population ratio.................................	57.7	58.4	61.5	62.8	54.1	54.3
Unemployed..	9,130	7,559	5,348	4,309	3,782	3,250
Unemployment rate...	7.0	5.8	7.9	6.4	6.1	5.2
Not in labor force...	79,291	79,663	33,535	33,301	45,756	46,362

NOTE: The foreign born are those residing in the United States who were not U.S. citizens at birth. That is, they were born outside the United States or one of its outlying areas such as Puerto Rico or Guam, to parents neither of whom was a U.S. citizen. The native born are persons who were born in the United States or one of its outlying areas such as Puerto Rico or Guam or who were born abroad of at least one parent who was a U.S. citizen. Updated population controls are introduced annually with the release of January data.

Table A-8. Employed persons by class of worker and part-time status

[In thousands]

Category	Not seasonally adjusted			Seasonally adjusted					
	Feb. 2014	Jan. 2015	Feb. 2015	Feb. 2014	Oct. 2014	Nov. 2014	Dec. 2014	Jan. 2015	Feb. 2015
CLASS OF WORKER									
Agriculture and related industries..................	1,973	2,234	2,234	2,148	2,402	2,392	2,358	2,419	2,430
Wage and salary workers[1]......................	1,225	1,410	1,397	1,379	1,581	1,621	1,506	1,566	1,572
Self-employed workers, unincorporated.......	732	802	808	765	784	749	815	835	833
Unpaid family workers...........................	16	22	29	–	–	–	–	–	–
Nonagricultural industries..........................	142,160	144,317	144,884	143,196	144,982	144,939	145,101	145,743	145,880
Wage and salary workers[1]......................	133,551	135,748	136,577	134,482	136,016	136,093	136,415	136,949	137,447
Government....................................	20,517	20,555	20,893	20,255	19,885	19,956	19,956	20,330	20,582
Private industries..............................	113,033	115,193	115,683	114,239	116,059	116,144	116,469	116,664	116,890
Private households.........................	822	937	817	–	–	–	–	–	–
Other industries.............................	112,211	114,257	114,866	113,388	115,281	115,361	115,676	115,724	116,042
Self-employed workers, unincorporated.......	8,529	8,512	8,238	8,693	8,908	8,794	8,660	8,725	8,386
Unpaid family workers...........................	81	57	69	–	–	–	–	–	–
PERSONS AT WORK PART TIME[2]									
All industries									
Part time for economic reasons[3]..................	7,397	7,269	6,772	7,204	7,012	6,851	6,790	6,810	6,635
Slack work or business conditions.............	4,506	4,450	4,011	4,259	4,215	4,068	4,061	4,012	3,847
Could only find part-time work..................	2,598	2,353	2,355	2,674	2,437	2,447	2,432	2,460	2,426
Part time for noneconomic reasons[4]..............	19,651	20,033	20,437	19,085	19,793	19,971	19,730	19,822	19,837
Nonagricultural industries									
Part time for economic reasons[3]..................	7,269	7,125	6,669	7,091	6,911	6,731	6,699	6,690	6,539
Slack work or business conditions.............	4,449	4,372	3,941	4,222	4,149	3,997	3,983	3,951	3,791
Could only find part-time work..................	2,565	2,338	2,345	2,638	2,407	2,412	2,411	2,432	2,415
Part time for noneconomic reasons[4]..............	19,290	19,681	20,079	18,723	19,443	19,594	19,416	19,446	19,505

[1] Includes self-employed workers whose businesses are incorporated.

[2] Refers to those who worked 1 to 34 hours during the survey reference week and excludes employed persons who were absent from their jobs for the entire week.

[3] Refers to those who worked 1 to 34 hours during the reference week for an economic reason such as slack work or unfavorable business conditions, inability to find full-time work, or seasonal declines in demand.

[4] Refers to persons who usually work part time for noneconomic reasons such as childcare problems, family or personal obligations, school or training, retirement or Social Security limits on earnings, and other reasons. This excludes persons who usually work full time but worked only 1 to 34 hours during the reference week for reasons such as vacations, holidays, illness, and bad weather.

- Data not available.

NOTE: Detail for the seasonally adjusted data shown in this table will not necessarily add to totals because of the independent seasonal adjustment of the various series. Updated population controls are introduced annually with the release of January data.

Table A-9. Selected employment indicators

[Numbers in thousands]

Characteristic	Not seasonally adjusted			Seasonally adjusted					
	Feb. 2014	Jan. 2015	Feb. 2015	Feb. 2014	Oct. 2014	Nov. 2014	Dec. 2014	Jan. 2015	Feb. 2015
AGE AND SEX									
Total, 16 years and over.............................	144,134	146,552	147,118	145,301	147,260	147,331	147,442	148,201	148,297
16 to 19 years...	3,933	4,294	4,389	4,312	4,772	4,762	4,784	4,722	4,808
16 to 17 years......................................	1,309	1,474	1,433	1,492	1,626	1,663	1,678	1,651	1,637
18 to 19 years......................................	2,624	2,819	2,956	2,841	3,141	3,065	3,090	3,058	3,186
20 years and over..................................	140,201	142,258	142,729	140,989	142,488	142,569	142,658	143,480	143,489
20 to 24 years......................................	13,424	13,618	13,833	13,715	14,088	13,939	13,847	14,011	14,114
25 years and over..................................	126,777	128,640	128,896	127,307	128,522	128,673	128,860	129,435	129,349
25 to 54 years..................................	94,666	95,834	96,086	95,242	95,772	95,856	95,975	96,464	96,565
25 to 34 years..............................	31,673	32,309	32,559	31,856	32,228	32,271	32,354	32,574	32,682
35 to 44 years..............................	30,840	31,005	30,909	31,003	30,994	31,018	31,021	31,157	31,071
45 to 54 years..............................	32,154	32,520	32,618	32,382	32,550	32,567	32,600	32,734	32,812
55 years and over..............................	32,111	32,806	32,810	32,065	32,750	32,817	32,885	32,971	32,784
Men, 16 years and over...........................	75,687	77,477	77,824	76,852	78,286	78,084	78,400	78,869	79,006
16 to 19 years...	1,805	2,113	2,153	2,032	2,358	2,409	2,374	2,372	2,418
16 to 17 years......................................	568	692	666	667	785	847	828	802	791
18 to 19 years......................................	1,237	1,420	1,487	1,376	1,584	1,552	1,531	1,560	1,636
20 years and over..................................	73,882	75,364	75,671	74,820	75,928	75,675	76,026	76,496	76,588
20 to 24 years......................................	6,791	6,915	7,102	7,021	7,337	7,114	7,167	7,198	7,324
25 years and over..................................	67,092	68,449	68,569	67,757	68,673	68,593	68,890	69,248	69,190
25 to 54 years..................................	50,232	51,186	51,312	50,827	51,327	51,282	51,448	51,809	51,860
25 to 34 years..............................	17,004	17,458	17,560	17,214	17,367	17,336	17,534	17,722	17,743
35 to 44 years..............................	16,455	16,641	16,595	16,622	16,802	16,784	16,748	16,807	16,760
45 to 54 years..............................	16,773	17,087	17,157	16,991	17,159	17,162	17,166	17,281	17,357
55 years and over..............................	16,860	17,263	17,256	16,930	17,346	17,311	17,441	17,439	17,330
Women, 16 years and over........................	68,446	69,075	69,294	68,449	68,974	69,247	69,042	69,332	69,291
16 to 19 years...	2,128	2,181	2,236	2,281	2,414	2,353	2,410	2,349	2,389
16 to 17 years......................................	740	782	767	825	841	816	850	849	846
18 to 19 years......................................	1,388	1,399	1,470	1,465	1,557	1,513	1,559	1,499	1,550
20 years and over..................................	66,319	66,894	67,058	66,168	66,560	66,894	66,632	66,983	66,901
20 to 24 years......................................	6,633	6,703	6,731	6,694	6,751	6,825	6,680	6,813	6,790
25 years and over..................................	59,685	60,191	60,328	59,551	59,849	60,080	59,970	60,187	60,159
25 to 54 years..................................	44,435	44,648	44,774	44,415	44,445	44,574	44,527	44,655	44,705
25 to 34 years..............................	14,669	14,852	14,999	14,642	14,861	14,935	14,820	14,852	14,939
35 to 44 years..............................	14,385	14,364	14,314	14,381	14,192	14,234	14,273	14,350	14,311
45 to 54 years..............................	15,381	15,432	15,461	15,392	15,391	15,406	15,434	15,453	15,456
55 years and over..............................	15,251	15,543	15,553	15,136	15,404	15,506	15,443	15,532	15,453
MARITAL STATUS									
Married men, spouse present..........................	43,889	44,555	44,575	44,281	44,380	44,267	44,588	44,934	44,951
Married women, spouse present......................	34,874	34,929	35,146	34,664	34,833	34,799	34,645	34,843	34,910
Women who maintain families........................	9,333	9,300	9,137	–	–	–	–	–	–
FULL- OR PART-TIME STATUS									
Full-time workers[1].....................................	116,323	118,840	119,313	117,859	119,681	119,507	119,934	120,711	120,834
Part-time workers[2].....................................	27,810	27,712	27,805	27,382	27,690	27,775	27,506	27,546	27,471
MULTIPLE JOBHOLDERS									
Total multiple jobholders.............................	7,163	7,289	7,221	6,989	7,674	7,403	7,285	7,485	7,059
Percent of total employed............................	5.0	5.0	4.9	4.8	5.2	5.0	4.9	5.1	4.8
SELF-EMPLOYMENT									
Self-employed workers, incorporated..................	5,385	5,483	5,425	–	–	–	–	–	–
Self-employed workers, unincorporated................	9,261	9,315	9,047	9,458	9,692	9,543	9,475	9,560	9,220

[1] Employed full-time workers are persons who usually work 35 hours or more per week.
[2] Employed part-time workers are persons who usually work less than 35 hours per week.
- Data not available.
NOTE: Detail for the seasonally adjusted data shown in this table will not necessarily add to totals because of the independent seasonal adjustment of the various series. Updated population controls are introduced annually with the release of January data.

HOUSEHOLD DATA
Table A-10. Selected unemployment indicators, seasonally adjusted

Characteristic	Number of unemployed persons (in thousands)			Unemployment rates					
	Feb. 2014	Jan. 2015	Feb. 2015	Feb. 2014	Oct. 2014	Nov. 2014	Dec. 2014	Jan. 2015	Feb. 2015
AGE AND SEX									
Total, 16 years and over............................	10,387	8,979	8,705	6.7	5.7	5.8	5.6	5.7	5.5
16 to 19 years.....................................	1,168	1,096	993	21.3	18.7	17.5	16.8	18.8	17.1
16 to 17 years.................................	416	411	374	21.8	22.3	17.8	18.8	19.9	18.6
18 to 19 years.................................	747	678	625	20.8	16.8	17.6	15.4	18.2	16.4
20 years and over................................	9,219	7,883	7,712	6.1	5.2	5.4	5.1	5.2	5.1
20 to 24 years..................................	1,850	1,517	1,563	11.9	10.5	10.9	10.8	9.8	10.0
25 years and over..............................	7,325	6,273	6,124	5.4	4.7	4.7	4.5	4.6	4.5
25 to 54 years...............................	5,764	4,870	4,634	5.7	4.9	4.8	4.7	4.8	4.6
25 to 34 years............................	2,409	2,029	1,869	7.0	6.2	6.1	5.9	5.9	5.4
35 to 44 years............................	1,655	1,436	1,452	5.1	4.4	4.3	4.3	4.4	4.5
45 to 54 years............................	1,700	1,405	1,312	5.0	4.0	4.1	4.0	4.1	3.8
55 years and over...........................	1,551	1,417	1,479	4.6	4.1	4.5	3.9	4.1	4.3
Men, 16 years and over............................	5,714	4,903	4,766	6.9	5.6	5.9	5.8	5.9	5.7
16 to 19 years.....................................	650	595	523	24.2	19.5	17.8	19.2	20.0	17.8
16 to 17 years.................................	218	211	188	24.7	25.5	20.1	20.0	20.8	19.2
18 to 19 years.................................	432	374	343	23.9	16.7	16.6	18.2	19.4	17.3
20 years and over................................	5,064	4,308	4,243	6.3	5.1	5.4	5.3	5.3	5.2
20 to 24 years..................................	1,085	933	891	13.4	10.4	11.8	11.6	11.5	10.9
25 years and over..............................	3,921	3,325	3,321	5.5	4.6	4.8	4.6	4.6	4.6
25 to 54 years...............................	3,090	2,571	2,494	5.7	4.7	4.8	4.7	4.7	4.6
25 to 34 years............................	1,275	1,092	1,045	6.9	6.0	6.0	5.7	5.8	5.6
35 to 44 years............................	893	780	753	5.1	4.1	4.2	4.3	4.4	4.3
45 to 54 years............................	922	699	696	5.1	3.8	4.1	4.1	3.9	3.9
55 years and over...........................	831	754	827	4.7	4.3	4.7	4.2	4.1	4.6
Women, 16 years and over........................	4,673	4,076	3,939	6.4	5.9	5.7	5.3	5.6	5.4
16 to 19 years.....................................	518	501	470	18.5	17.8	17.2	14.2	17.6	16.4
16 to 17 years.................................	197	200	186	19.3	19.0	15.2	17.6	19.0	18.0
18 to 19 years.................................	316	304	282	17.7	17.0	18.6	12.4	16.9	15.4
20 years and over................................	4,155	3,575	3,469	5.9	5.4	5.2	5.0	5.1	4.9
20 to 24 years..................................	764	584	671	10.2	10.7	10.0	9.9	7.9	9.0
25 years and over..............................	3,404	2,949	2,803	5.4	4.8	4.7	4.4	4.7	4.5
25 to 54 years...............................	2,673	2,299	2,140	5.7	5.2	4.9	4.7	4.9	4.6
25 to 34 years............................	1,134	937	824	7.2	6.4	6.1	6.0	5.9	5.2
35 to 44 years............................	762	655	699	5.0	4.8	4.6	4.3	4.4	4.7
45 to 54 years............................	778	706	617	4.8	4.3	4.0	3.9	4.4	3.8
55 years and over...........................	710	670	644	4.5	3.7	4.2	3.7	4.1	4.0
MARITAL STATUS									
Married men, spouse present.....................	1,735	1,356	1,405	3.8	3.0	3.2	3.0	2.9	3.0
Married women, spouse present..................	1,520	1,206	1,167	4.2	3.5	3.4	3.2	3.3	3.2
Women who maintain families[1]...................	935	824	760	9.1	8.7	8.2	7.8	8.1	7.7
FULL- OR PART-TIME STATUS									
Full-time workers[2].................................	8,783	7,525	7,275	6.9	6.0	6.0	5.7	5.9	5.7
Part-time workers[3]................................	1,609	1,433	1,405	5.6	5.0	5.1	5.0	4.9	4.9

[1] Not seasonally adjusted.

[2] Full-time workers are unemployed persons who have expressed a desire to work full time (35 hours or more per week) or are on layoff from full-time jobs.

[3] Part-time workers are unemployed persons who have expressed a desire to work part time (less than 35 hours per week) or are on layoff from part-time jobs.

NOTE: Detail for the seasonally adjusted data shown in this table will not necessarily add to totals because of the independent seasonal adjustment of the various series. Updated population controls are introduced annually with the release of January data.

Table A-11. Unemployed persons by reason for unemployment

[Numbers in thousands]

Reason	Not seasonally adjusted			Seasonally adjusted					
	Feb. 2014	Jan. 2015	Feb. 2015	Feb. 2014	Oct. 2014	Nov. 2014	Dec. 2014	Jan. 2015	Feb. 2015
NUMBER OF UNEMPLOYED									
Job losers and persons who completed temporary jobs.................	6,024	4,912	4,721	5,403	4,349	4,480	4,325	4,242	4,180
On temporary layoff..........................	1,341	1,328	1,349	1,037	847	1,070	959	902	1,021
Not on temporary layoff....................	4,682	3,584	3,372	4,366	3,501	3,410	3,366	3,339	3,158
Permanent job losers.....................	3,366	2,491	2,316	3,190	2,505	2,446	2,388	2,371	2,212
Persons who completed temporary jobs....	1,316	1,093	1,056	1,177	997	964	977	968	946
Job leavers......................................	813	868	894	816	782	835	798	851	884
Reentrants......................................	2,974	2,832	2,635	2,972	2,856	2,761	2,701	2,829	2,655
New entrants...................................	1,083	885	845	1,232	1,058	1,045	971	1,033	972
PERCENT DISTRIBUTION									
Job losers and persons who completed temporary jobs.................	55.3	51.7	51.9	51.8	48.1	49.1	49.2	47.4	48.1
On temporary layoff..........................	12.3	14.0	14.8	10.0	9.4	11.7	10.9	10.1	11.7
Not on temporary layoff....................	43.0	37.7	37.1	41.9	38.7	37.4	38.3	37.3	36.3
Job leavers......................................	7.5	9.1	9.8	7.8	8.6	9.2	9.1	9.5	10.2
Reentrants......................................	27.3	29.8	29.0	28.5	31.6	30.3	30.7	31.6	30.5
New entrants...................................	9.9	9.3	9.3	11.8	11.7	11.5	11.0	11.5	11.2
UNEMPLOYED AS A PERCENT OF THE CIVILIAN LABOR FORCE									
Job losers and persons who completed temporary jobs.................	3.9	3.1	3.0	3.5	2.8	2.9	2.8	2.7	2.7
Job leavers......................................	0.5	0.6	0.6	0.5	0.5	0.5	0.5	0.5	0.6
Reentrants......................................	1.9	1.8	1.7	1.9	1.8	1.8	1.7	1.8	1.7
New entrants...................................	0.7	0.6	0.5	0.8	0.7	0.7	0.6	0.7	0.6

NOTE: Updated population controls are introduced annually with the release of January data.

HOUSEHOLD DATA

Table A-12. Unemployed persons by duration of unemployment

[Numbers in thousands]

Duration	Not seasonally adjusted			Seasonally adjusted					
	Feb. 2014	Jan. 2015	Feb. 2015	Feb. 2014	Oct. 2014	Nov. 2014	Dec. 2014	Jan. 2015	Feb. 2015
NUMBER OF UNEMPLOYED									
Less than 5 weeks.................................	2,145	2,780	2,185	2,388	2,455	2,505	2,375	2,383	2,431
5 to 14 weeks..	3,091	2,468	2,662	2,558	2,322	2,378	2,293	2,318	2,223
15 weeks and over.................................	5,657	4,250	4,248	5,402	4,321	4,225	4,059	4,180	4,044
15 to 26 weeks..................................	1,771	1,396	1,485	1,597	1,416	1,403	1,274	1,380	1,335
27 weeks and over..............................	3,886	2,853	2,763	3,804	2,904	2,822	2,785	2,800	2,709
Average (mean) duration, in weeks..............	36.3	30.3	31.1	36.9	32.9	33.0	32.8	32.3	31.7
Median duration, in weeks.........................	16.0	12.3	13.1	16.2	13.5	12.8	12.6	13.4	13.1
PERCENT DISTRIBUTION									
Less than 5 weeks.................................	19.7	29.3	24.0	23.1	27.0	27.5	27.2	26.8	27.9
5 to 14 weeks..	28.4	26.0	29.3	24.7	25.5	26.1	26.3	26.1	25.6
15 weeks and over.................................	51.9	44.7	46.7	52.2	47.5	46.4	46.5	47.1	46.5
15 to 26 weeks..................................	16.3	14.7	16.3	15.4	15.6	15.4	14.6	15.5	15.4
27 weeks and over..............................	35.7	30.0	30.4	36.8	31.9	31.0	31.9	31.5	31.1

NOTE: Updated population controls are introduced annually with the release of January data.

Table A-13. Employed and unemployed persons by occupation, not seasonally adjusted

[Numbers in thousands]

Occupation	Employed		Unemployed		Unemployment rates	
	Feb. 2014	Feb. 2015	Feb. 2014	Feb. 2015	Feb. 2014	Feb. 2015
Total, 16 years and over[1]..	144,134	147,118	10,893	9,095	7.0	5.8
Management, professional, and related occupations...........	55,501	57,596	1,845	1,601	3.2	2.7
Management, business, and financial operations occupations..	22,664	23,630	838	674	3.6	2.8
Professional and related occupations..........................	32,838	33,966	1,007	927	3.0	2.7
Service occupations...	25,007	24,802	2,249	1,971	8.3	7.4
Sales and office occupations.......................................	33,667	34,054	2,522	1,821	7.0	5.1
Sales and related occupations..................................	15,799	15,838	1,322	868	7.7	5.2
Office and administrative support occupations..............	17,868	18,216	1,200	953	6.3	5.0
Natural resources, construction, and maintenance occupations..	13,148	13,258	1,487	1,454	10.2	9.9
Farming, fishing, and forestry occupations...................	905	966	115	170	11.3	15.0
Construction and extraction occupations......................	7,409	7,323	1,114	959	13.1	11.6
Installation, maintenance, and repair occupations...........	4,833	4,968	257	325	5.0	6.1
Production, transportation, and material moving occupations..	16,811	17,409	1,671	1,380	9.0	7.3
Production occupations..	8,198	8,481	692	639	7.8	7.0
Transportation and material moving occupations............	8,613	8,928	978	741	10.2	7.7

[1] Persons with no previous work experience and persons whose last job was in the U.S. Armed Forces are included in the unemployed total.

NOTE: Updated population controls are introduced annually with the release of January data.

Table A-14. Unemployed persons by industry and class of worker, not seasonally adjusted

Industry and class of worker	Number of unemployed persons (in thousands)		Unemployment rates	
	Feb. 2014	Feb. 2015	Feb. 2014	Feb. 2015
Total, 16 years and over[1]	10,893	9,095	7.0	5.8
Nonagricultural private wage and salary workers	8,479	7,046	7.0	5.7
Mining, quarrying, and oil and gas extraction	98	90	8.0	8.6
Construction	1,098	906	12.8	10.6
Manufacturing	843	814	5.5	5.2
Durable goods	454	456	4.6	4.7
Nondurable goods	389	357	6.9	6.2
Wholesale and retail trade	1,571	1,193	7.6	5.7
Transportation and utilities	412	308	6.6	5.0
Information	145	130	4.8	4.5
Financial activities	400	292	4.2	3.1
Professional and business services	1,324	911	8.6	5.8
Education and health services	893	794	4.0	3.5
Leisure and hospitality	1,336	1,165	10.3	8.8
Other services	359	443	5.9	6.7
Agriculture and related private wage and salary workers	153	196	11.4	12.7
Government workers	683	513	3.2	2.4
Self-employed workers, unincorporated, and unpaid family workers	496	495	5.0	5.1

[1] Persons with no previous work experience and persons whose last job was in the U.S. Armed Forces are included in the unemployed total.
NOTE: Updated population controls are introduced annually with the release of January data.

Table A-15. Alternative measures of labor underutilization
[Percent]

Measure	Not seasonally adjusted			Seasonally adjusted					
	Feb. 2014	Jan. 2015	Feb. 2015	Feb. 2014	Oct. 2014	Nov. 2014	Dec. 2014	Jan. 2015	Feb. 2015
U-1 Persons unemployed 15 weeks or longer, as a percent of the civilian labor force.........	3.6	2.7	2.7	3.5	2.8	2.7	2.6	2.7	2.6
U-2 Job losers and persons who completed temporary jobs, as a percent of the civilian labor force.......................................	3.9	3.1	3.0	3.5	2.8	2.9	2.8	2.7	2.7
U-3 Total unemployed, as a percent of the civilian labor force (official unemployment rate)..	7.0	6.1	5.8	6.7	5.7	5.8	5.6	5.7	5.5
U-4 Total unemployed plus discouraged workers, as a percent of the civilian labor force plus discouraged workers.................	7.5	6.5	6.3	7.1	6.2	6.2	6.0	6.1	6.0
U-5 Total unemployed, plus discouraged workers, plus all other persons marginally attached to the labor force, as a percent of the civilian labor force plus all persons marginally attached to the labor force.........	8.4	7.4	7.1	8.0	7.1	7.1	6.9	7.0	6.8
U-6 Total unemployed, plus all persons marginally attached to the labor force, plus total employed part time for economic reasons, as a percent of the civilian labor force plus all persons marginally attached to the labor force......................................	13.1	12.0	11.4	12.6	11.5	11.4	11.2	11.3	11.0

NOTE: Persons marginally attached to the labor force are those who currently are neither working nor looking for work but indicate that they want and are available for a job and have looked for work sometime in the past 12 months. Discouraged workers, a subset of the marginally attached, have given a job-market related reason for not currently looking for work. Persons employed part time for economic reasons are those who want and are available for full-time work but have had to settle for a part-time schedule. Updated population controls are introduced annually with the release of January data.

Table A-16. Persons not in the labor force and multiple jobholders by sex, not seasonally adjusted

[Numbers in thousands]

Category	Total		Men		Women	
	Feb. 2014	Feb. 2015	Feb. 2014	Feb. 2015	Feb. 2014	Feb. 2015
NOT IN THE LABOR FORCE						
Total not in the labor force..	92,058	93,686	37,352	37,607	54,707	56,079
Persons who currently want a job................................	6,091	6,575	2,984	3,054	3,107	3,521
Marginally attached to the labor force[1]........................	2,303	2,159	1,295	1,108	1,008	1,052
Discouraged workers[2].......................................	755	732	466	430	289	302
Other persons marginally attached to the labor force[3]. ..	1,548	1,428	829	678	719	750
MULTIPLE JOBHOLDERS						
Total multiple jobholders[4]..	7,163	7,221	3,466	3,585	3,697	3,636
Percent of total employed..	5.0	4.9	4.6	4.6	5.4	5.2
Primary job full time, secondary job part time...................	3,702	3,824	1,974	2,105	1,728	1,720
Primary and secondary jobs both part time.....................	1,973	1,983	680	687	1,293	1,296
Primary and secondary jobs both full time......................	275	231	166	143	109	88
Hours vary on primary or secondary job........................	1,154	1,132	619	621	535	511

[1] Data refer to persons who want a job, have searched for work during the prior 12 months, and were available to take a job during the reference week, but had not looked for work in the past 4 weeks.

[2] Includes those who did not actively look for work in the prior 4 weeks for reasons such as thinks no work available, could not find work, lacks schooling or training, employer thinks too young or old, and other types of discrimination.

[3] Includes those who did not actively look for work in the prior 4 weeks for such reasons as school or family responsibilities, ill health, and transportation problems, as well as a number for whom reason for nonparticipation was not determined.

[4] Includes a small number of persons who work part time on their primary job and full time on their secondary job(s), not shown separately.

NOTE: Updated population controls are introduced annually with the release of January data.

Table B-1. Employees on nonfarm payrolls by industry sector and selected industry detail
[In thousands]

Industry	Not seasonally adjusted				Seasonally adjusted				Change from: Jan.2015 - Feb.2015P
	Feb. 2014	Dec. 2014	Jan. 2015P	Feb. 2015P	Feb. 2014	Dec. 2014	Jan. 2015P	Feb. 2015P	
Total nonfarm...	136,257	141,484	138,663	139,566	137,830	140,592	140,831	141,126	295
Total private..	114,147	119,223	116,898	117,365	116,006	118,690	118,927	119,215	288
Goods-producing..................................	18,491	19,389	19,033	19,050	19,031	19,489	19,553	19,582	29
Mining and logging............................	860	912	893	880	877	913	907	899	-8
Logging.....................................	49.9	53.6	52.9	52.5	51.6	53.0	53.5	54.1	0.6
Mining......................................	810.3	858.3	840.5	827.4	825.5	859.6	853.8	844.5	-9.3
Oil and gas extraction...............	194.5	201.9	199.2	197.1	195.4	201.2	199.4	198.3	-1.1
Mining, except oil and gas[1]........	199.7	203.7	197.9	196.5	208.7	207.0	206.6	205.8	-0.8
Coal mining..........................	74.8	72.1	70.9	70.2	74.9	72.0	71.4	70.7	-0.7
Support activities for mining..........	416.1	452.7	443.4	433.8	421.4	451.4	447.8	440.4	-7.4
Construction.......................................	5,612	6,175	5,926	5,935	6,032	6,275	6,324	6,353	29
Construction of buildings.......................	1,267.9	1,381.2	1,348.5	1,343.5	1,333.4	1,388.0	1,405.1	1,410.3	5.2
Residential building.......................	609.0	673.9	658.7	652.6	642.6	677.4	688.4	687.9	-0.5
Nonresidential building....................	658.9	707.3	689.8	690.9	690.8	710.6	716.7	722.4	5.7
Heavy and civil engineering construction......	793.5	897.6	833.6	830.2	899.7	932.7	939.1	935.4	-3.7
Specialty trade contractors...................	3,550.6	3,896.4	3,743.8	3,761.5	3,798.5	3,954.3	3,979.9	4,007.1	27.2
Residential specialty trade contractors......	1,509.9	1,685.8	1,616.8	1,628.9	1,625.4	1,719.2	1,730.7	1,747.9	17.2
Nonresidential specialty trade contractors...	2,040.7	2,210.6	2,127.0	2,132.6	2,173.1	2,235.1	2,249.2	2,259.2	10.0
Manufacturing....................................	12,019	12,302	12,214	12,235	12,122	12,301	12,322	12,330	8
Durable goods.................................	7,564	7,786	7,743	7,762	7,614	7,782	7,798	7,809	11
Wood products.............................	360.0	374.6	373.4	373.1	365.9	376.8	380.1	378.9	-1.2
Nonmetallic mineral products..............	361.8	392.6	382.0	382.1	377.1	396.3	396.8	397.7	0.9
Primary metals............................	395.1	408.2	407.5	406.8	397.1	407.9	407.8	408.1	0.3
Fabricated metal products..................	1,436.6	1,474.6	1,464.9	1,469.2	1,446.9	1,473.3	1,475.3	1,478.0	2.7
Machinery.................................	1,111.7	1,143.7	1,142.0	1,145.1	1,113.5	1,144.0	1,146.1	1,147.8	1.7
Computer and electronic products[1]........	1,046.4	1,055.6	1,052.7	1,055.0	1,050.5	1,054.8	1,056.6	1,059.0	2.4
Computer and peripheral equipment......	158.2	168.3	167.6	168.0	158.9	167.8	167.9	168.5	0.6
Communications equipment..............	95.2	91.7	90.2	90.2	95.4	91.4	90.2	90.5	0.3
Semiconductors and electronic components..............................	369.0	369.2	369.5	370.4	369.9	369.1	371.0	371.4	0.4
Electronic instruments....................	386.6	388.0	387.5	389.7	388.5	388.7	389.6	391.5	1.9
Electrical equipment and appliances........	376.0	372.6	371.0	371.8	376.5	371.8	371.8	372.5	0.7
Transportation equipment[1]...............	1,537.0	1,595.7	1,587.6	1,596.0	1,539.7	1,591.0	1,594.6	1,596.8	2.2
Motor vehicles and parts[2]...............	858.4	907.6	903.2	906.7	858.8	902.5	906.3	907.1	0.8
Furniture and related products.............	361.1	382.0	379.1	380.2	365.8	382.6	384.2	385.4	1.2
Miscellaneous durable goods manufacturing.............................	578.6	586.1	582.4	582.2	581.0	583.9	584.7	584.7	0.0
Nondurable goods.............................	4,455	4,516	4,471	4,473	4,508	4,519	4,524	4,521	-3
Food manufacturing........................	1,463.0	1,483.6	1,465.0	1,468.2	1,492.9	1,484.6	1,493.5	1,494.5	1.0
Textile mills..............................	116.7	118.3	117.7	118.5	117.4	118.3	119.4	119.1	-0.3
Textile product mills......................	111.9	116.9	112.9	113.3	113.3	115.9	114.6	114.8	0.2
Apparel..................................	143.1	138.4	138.7	138.0	142.5	137.8	138.3	137.0	-1.3
Paper and paper products.................	372.8	368.2	365.2	363.8	374.7	367.6	366.1	365.4	-0.7
Printing and related support activities.......	451.4	452.2	444.6	445.6	453.7	450.2	447.2	447.8	0.6
Petroleum and coal products..............	106.5	109.6	108.4	102.8	110.3	111.7	112.2	106.5	-5.7
Chemicals................................	795.0	811.6	806.3	809.5	797.0	811.6	808.6	811.3	2.7
Plastics and rubber products..............	668.2	681.6	679.9	681.2	672.3	682.6	684.1	684.7	0.6
Miscellaneous nondurable goods manufacturing.............................	226.7	235.9	232.6	231.9	234.1	238.9	239.6	239.4	-0.2
Private service-providing...........................	95,656	99,834	97,865	98,315	96,975	99,201	99,374	99,633	259
Trade, transportation, and utilities................	25,743	27,402	26,540	26,384	26,141	26,669	26,713	26,775	62
Wholesale trade...............................	5,738.9	5,882.1	5,837.6	5,853.7	5,787.8	5,875.5	5,889.5	5,901.2	11.7
Durable goods............................	2,872.9	2,936.4	2,922.5	2,930.1	2,889.7	2,935.4	2,940.2	2,947.3	7.1
Nondurable goods........................	1,984.1	2,031.3	2,010.3	2,017.7	2,009.2	2,031.1	2,036.3	2,041.3	5.0
Electronic markets and agents and brokers..................................	881.9	914.4	904.8	905.9	888.9	909.0	913.0	912.6	-0.4
Retail trade...................................	14,946.1	16,058.6	15,428.5	15,260.2	15,238.2	15,497.3	15,525.1	15,557.1	32.0
Motor vehicle and parts dealers[1]...........	1,811.9	1,882.3	1,874.6	1,884.4	1,838.0	1,894.0	1,902.5	1,907.7	5.2
Automobile dealers......................	1,159.9	1,203.7	1,200.8	1,204.8	1,170.1	1,208.1	1,211.6	1,213.4	1.8

See footnotes at end of table.

Table B-1. Employees on nonfarm payrolls by industry sector and selected industry detail — Continued

[In thousands]

Industry	Not seasonally adjusted				Seasonally adjusted				
	Feb. 2014	Dec. 2014	Jan. 2015[p]	Feb. 2015[p]	Feb. 2014	Dec. 2014	Jan. 2015[p]	Feb. 2015[p]	Change from: Jan.2015 - Feb.2015[p]
Retail trade - Continued									
Furniture and home furnishings stores......	445.4	482.4	462.3	458.9	450.1	457.4	460.0	464.1	4.1
Electronics and appliance stores...........	489.4	523.3	514.0	489.6	492.8	491.9	493.6	492.7	-0.9
Building material and garden supply stores...................................	1,175.7	1,208.6	1,184.5	1,205.5	1,226.5	1,246.6	1,250.5	1,256.2	5.7
Food and beverage stores.................	2,940.8	3,049.2	3,011.2	2,996.0	2,972.1	3,020.5	3,026.1	3,029.0	2.9
Health and personal care stores...........	1,004.8	1,045.5	1,031.2	1,022.4	1,008.9	1,025.9	1,028.1	1,027.2	-0.9
Gasoline stations.........................	858.4	886.1	881.7	881.0	875.3	889.1	893.6	896.5	2.9
Clothing and clothing accessories stores....	1,328.0	1,536.2	1,375.9	1,326.5	1,380.4	1,370.7	1,369.4	1,377.0	7.6
Sporting goods, hobby, book, and music stores...................................	588.8	688.3	613.5	601.9	603.9	626.2	616.0	620.2	4.2
General merchandise stores[1]...............	3,025.8	3,368.5	3,157.3	3,076.2	3,092.2	3,138.6	3,142.9	3,143.7	0.8
Department stores.......................	1,318.7	1,501.6	1,365.9	1,307.3	1,349.8	1,342.8	1,342.2	1,339.3	-2.9
Miscellaneous store retailers...............	797.0	836.1	802.9	802.3	809.6	821.7	821.7	818.1	-3.6
Nonstore retailers........................	480.1	552.1	519.4	515.5	488.4	514.7	520.7	524.7	4.0
Transportation and warehousing...............	4,511.6	4,903.7	4,716.5	4,713.6	4,565.8	4,738.5	4,739.5	4,758.0	18.5
Air transportation........................	437.0	442.0	442.0	441.4	440.2	443.3	444.3	444.6	0.3
Rail transportation.......................	229.6	241.4	239.4	239.8	231.3	241.3	240.4	241.2	0.8
Water transportation.....................	65.2	66.8	65.0	64.8	66.9	67.4	66.9	66.5	-0.4
Truck transportation......................	1,361.2	1,437.6	1,413.8	1,413.6	1,395.3	1,441.1	1,443.6	1,446.2	2.6
Transit and ground passenger transportation.........................	473.0	488.6	485.1	482.0	460.0	471.1	472.2	469.6	-2.6
Pipeline transportation....................	46.4	47.6	47.3	47.9	46.3	47.6	47.4	47.8	0.4
Scenic and sightseeing transportation.......	23.1	25.9	23.7	24.6	30.0	30.6	31.0	31.3	0.3
Support activities for transportation.........	611.6	636.8	630.0	630.3	614.0	632.3	631.8	632.7	0.9
Couriers and messengers..................	545.6	752.1	628.2	625.5	553.2	616.6	612.8	625.1	12.3
Warehousing and storage..................	718.9	764.9	742.0	743.7	728.6	747.2	749.1	753.0	3.9
Utilities....................................	546.8	557.2	557.1	556.4	549.1	557.9	558.4	558.8	0.4
Information.................................	2,707	2,775	2,737	2,770	2,720	2,767	2,772	2,779	7
Publishing industries, except Internet..........	723.8	724.8	718.4	717.3	727.3	721.4	721.2	720.5	-0.7
Motion picture and sound recording industries...............................	371.5	377.5	351.1	386.3	378.3	381.4	380.6	388.5	7.9
Broadcasting, except Internet.................	281.0	288.9	284.9	285.3	282.2	287.5	286.3	286.5	0.2
Telecommunications.........................	849.0	865.6	861.0	861.0	847.8	861.5	860.8	860.7	-0.1
Data processing, hosting and related services...............................	273.3	288.2	288.9	290.2	274.8	286.5	290.2	291.7	1.5
Other information services...................	208.2	229.9	233.0	230.0	209.5	228.5	232.5	231.3	-1.2
Financial activities...........................	7,879	8,059	8,018	8,029	7,931	8,049	8,071	8,081	10
Finance and insurance.......................	5,896.7	5,994.8	5,988.9	5,994.6	5,907.9	5,978.9	5,997.8	6,004.7	6.9
Monetary authorities - central bank..........	18.3	18.5	18.4	18.4	18.5	18.5	18.6	18.6	0.0
Credit intermediation and related activities[1]................................	2,571.0	2,573.6	2,567.4	2,563.3	2,575.3	2,565.9	2,568.6	2,567.0	-1.6
Depository credit intermediation[1]..........	1,715.2	1,702.2	1,701.5	1,696.6	1,717.3	1,700.2	1,699.9	1,698.3	-1.6
Commercial banking....................	1,301.8	1,285.7	1,285.8	1,281.6	1,302.4	1,284.5	1,283.8	1,281.7	-2.1
Securities, commodity contracts, investments, and funds and trusts........	872.3	888.6	889.9	892.5	873.9	888.0	893.1	894.3	1.2
Insurance carriers and related activities.....	2,435.1	2,514.1	2,513.2	2,520.4	2,440.2	2,506.5	2,517.5	2,524.8	7.3
Real estate and rental and leasing...........	1,982.4	2,064.2	2,028.8	2,034.8	2,023.2	2,070.5	2,072.9	2,076.5	3.6
Real estate...............................	1,451.6	1,503.5	1,479.3	1,482.7	1,474.9	1,501.2	1,504.0	1,506.1	2.1
Rental and leasing services................	507.5	536.9	526.7	529.2	524.7	545.9	545.6	547.2	1.6
Lessors of nonfinancial intangible assets....	23.3	23.8	22.8	22.9	23.6	23.4	23.3	23.2	-0.1
Professional and business services..............	18,562	19,519	19,112	19,228	18,840	19,439	19,449	19,500	51
Professional and technical services[1]..........	8,303.8	8,526.7	8,510.3	8,601.8	8,241.6	8,489.5	8,506.2	8,538.0	31.8
Legal services............................	1,114.6	1,124.2	1,109.8	1,114.7	1,121.8	1,120.0	1,118.2	1,121.3	3.1
Accounting and bookkeeping services......	1,069.1	981.3	1,059.5	1,117.0	941.7	980.9	982.1	988.2	6.1
Architectural and engineering services......	1,339.5	1,403.3	1,391.3	1,392.6	1,359.5	1,403.9	1,408.7	1,413.6	4.9
Computer systems design and related services................................	1,743.3	1,818.9	1,817.3	1,821.6	1,748.8	1,814.4	1,821.8	1,827.0	5.2
Management and technical consulting services................................	1,203.8	1,295.4	1,266.6	1,279.0	1,214.8	1,280.1	1,283.8	1,290.9	7.1
Management of companies and enterprises. ..	2,138.1	2,195.0	2,180.6	2,179.3	2,150.2	2,190.5	2,187.1	2,191.0	3.9

See footnotes at end of table.

Table B-1. Employees on nonfarm payrolls by industry sector and selected industry detail — Continued

[In thousands]

Industry	Not seasonally adjusted				Seasonally adjusted				Change from: Jan.2015 - Feb.2015[p]
	Feb. 2014	Dec. 2014	Jan. 2015[p]	Feb. 2015[p]	Feb. 2014	Dec. 2014	Jan. 2015[p]	Feb. 2015[p]	
Professional and business services - Continued									
Administrative and waste services............	8,119.6	8,797.1	8,421.5	8,446.8	8,448.4	8,759.4	8,755.2	8,771.1	15.9
Administrative and support services[1]........	7,747.0	8,412.0	8,039.7	8,064.9	8,066.7	8,370.4	8,366.6	8,380.5	13.9
Employment services[1]....................	3,198.0	3,638.5	3,377.6	3,384.7	3,334.7	3,537.7	3,521.9	3,520.5	-1.4
Temporary help services...............	2,580.0	2,957.9	2,731.1	2,726.6	2,700.6	2,863.3	2,849.5	2,841.7	-7.8
Business support services...............	875.2	926.6	906.8	908.2	873.7	900.3	903.4	905.9	2.5
Services to buildings and dwellings.......	1,765.8	1,871.2	1,797.8	1,801.7	1,929.2	1,952.0	1,961.6	1,964.3	2.7
Waste management and remediation services.................................	372.6	385.1	381.8	381.9	381.7	389.0	388.6	390.6	2.0
Education and health services..................	21,374	21,893	21,634	21,916	21,279	21,718	21,764	21,818	54
Educational services...........................	3,529.8	3,545.3	3,342.9	3,595.1	3,389.5	3,439.9	3,433.8	3,455.1	21.3
Health care and social assistance............	17,844.6	18,347.4	18,291.1	18,321.3	17,889.3	18,277.7	18,330.2	18,363.0	32.8
Health care[3].................................	14,522.3	14,914.6	14,865.4	14,881.6	14,572.0	14,863.7	14,903.8	14,927.6	23.8
Ambulatory health care services[1].........	6,532.8	6,794.5	6,771.0	6,787.8	6,556.9	6,766.9	6,788.5	6,808.4	19.9
Offices of physicians....................	2,441.8	2,516.6	2,513.8	2,518.4	2,448.9	2,501.8	2,515.2	2,522.5	7.3
Outpatient care centers.................	696.9	728.6	728.1	728.3	697.8	726.5	729.0	728.8	-0.2
Home health care services.............	1,233.6	1,297.5	1,284.9	1,285.6	1,241.2	1,289.6	1,291.5	1,294.7	3.2
Hospitals....................................	4,758.1	4,825.9	4,820.0	4,828.9	4,766.5	4,815.6	4,827.4	4,836.1	8.7
Nursing and residential care facilities[1]....	3,231.4	3,294.2	3,274.4	3,264.9	3,248.6	3,281.2	3,287.9	3,283.1	-4.8
Nursing care facilities...................	1,641.0	1,657.2	1,649.6	1,643.2	1,651.2	1,653.4	1,656.8	1,653.6	-3.2
Social assistance[1].........................	3,322.3	3,432.8	3,425.7	3,439.7	3,317.3	3,414.0	3,426.4	3,435.4	9.0
Child day care services..................	859.1	874.0	872.0	875.9	845.1	860.4	862.3	861.9	-0.4
Leisure and hospitality...........................	13,908	14,597	14,274	14,415	14,526	14,948	14,987	15,053	66
Arts, entertainment, and recreation............	1,873.8	1,967.2	1,892.9	1,923.5	2,080.0	2,133.2	2,129.1	2,135.3	6.2
Performing arts and spectator sports........	405.1	440.6	406.6	423.2	436.3	459.3	454.5	456.9	2.4
Museums, historical sites, and similar institutions..................................	134.0	138.5	133.7	133.0	144.9	145.2	145.4	144.3	-1.1
Amusements, gambling, and recreation.....	1,334.7	1,388.1	1,352.6	1,367.3	1,498.8	1,528.7	1,529.2	1,534.1	4.9
Accommodation and food services............	12,034.0	12,629.3	12,380.8	12,491.9	12,446.2	12,814.7	12,857.6	12,917.8	60.2
Accommodation............................	1,791.8	1,829.1	1,802.7	1,816.2	1,881.8	1,896.9	1,902.4	1,903.9	1.5
Food services and drinking places..........	10,242.2	10,800.2	10,578.1	10,675.7	10,564.4	10,917.8	10,955.2	11,013.9	58.7
Other services.................................	5,483	5,589	5,550	5,573	5,538	5,611	5,618	5,627	9
Repair and maintenance......................	1,217.7	1,243.0	1,244.1	1,256.3	1,230.0	1,253.3	1,259.6	1,267.2	7.6
Personal and laundry services................	1,337.5	1,380.9	1,365.6	1,363.1	1,354.3	1,380.7	1,383.4	1,380.6	-2.8
Membership associations and organizations...	2,927.5	2,965.3	2,940.0	2,953.8	2,953.3	2,976.5	2,975.0	2,978.8	3.8
Government..	22,110	22,261	21,765	22,201	21,824	21,902	21,904	21,911	7
Federal...	2,712.0	2,744.0	2,717.0	2,716.0	2,730.0	2,732.0	2,730.0	2,730.0	0.0
Federal, except U.S. Postal Service.............	2,124.6	2,133.0	2,124.8	2,122.9	2,139.7	2,134.6	2,138.3	2,135.2	-3.1
U.S. Postal Service.............................	587.6	611.3	592.6	593.1	590.5	597.6	591.4	595.0	3.6
State government.................................	5,182.0	5,194.0	4,984.0	5,211.0	5,061.0	5,079.0	5,080.0	5,083.0	3.0
State government education....................	2,539.7	2,555.0	2,350.5	2,578.4	2,408.0	2,430.5	2,434.3	2,438.7	4.4
State government, excluding education..........	2,642.5	2,639.1	2,633.8	2,632.6	2,652.6	2,648.9	2,646.0	2,644.1	-1.9
Local government.................................	14,216.0	14,323.0	14,064.0	14,274.0	14,033.0	14,091.0	14,094.0	14,098.0	4.0
Local government education....................	8,069.7	8,109.7	7,901.8	8,101.2	7,765.4	7,796.7	7,799.0	7,800.2	1.2
Local government, excluding education..........	6,145.9	6,213.5	6,161.9	6,172.7	6,267.7	6,294.1	6,294.9	6,297.5	2.6

[1] Includes other industries, not shown separately.
[2] Includes motor vehicles, motor vehicle bodies and trailers, and motor vehicle parts.
[3] Includes ambulatory health care services, hospitals, and nursing and residential care facilities.
p Preliminary
NOTE: Data have been revised to reflect March 2014 benchmark levels and updated seasonal adjustment factors.

ESTABLISHMENT DATA

Table B-2. Average weekly hours and overtime of all employees on private nonfarm payrolls by industry sector, seasonally adjusted

Industry	Feb. 2014	Dec. 2014	Jan. 2015[p]	Feb. 2015[p]
AVERAGE WEEKLY HOURS				
Total private...	34.4	34.6	34.6	34.6
Goods-producing...	40.3	40.6	40.5	40.7
Mining and logging..	45.1	44.9	44.7	44.6
Construction..	38.5	39.2	39.0	39.6
Manufacturing...	40.8	40.9	41.0	41.0
Durable goods..	41.3	41.4	41.5	41.4
Nondurable goods..	40.0	40.2	40.2	40.3
Private service-providing..	33.2	33.4	33.4	33.4
Trade, transportation, and utilities.................................	34.3	34.6	34.6	34.6
Wholesale trade...	38.7	38.9	38.9	38.9
Retail trade..	31.1	31.4	31.4	31.4
Transportation and warehousing...............................	38.6	39.0	38.8	38.9
Utilities..	42.2	42.2	42.3	42.2
Information...	36.8	36.3	36.5	36.5
Financial activities..	37.2	37.4	37.4	37.4
Professional and business services...............................	36.1	36.3	36.2	36.2
Education and health services.......................................	32.7	32.7	32.8	32.8
Leisure and hospitality..	26.1	26.3	26.4	26.4
Other services..	31.7	31.8	31.9	31.9
AVERAGE OVERTIME HOURS				
Manufacturing..	3.4	3.6	3.5	3.4
Durable goods...	3.4	3.6	3.5	3.4
Nondurable goods..	3.3	3.5	3.4	3.4

p Preliminary

NOTE: Data have been revised to reflect March 2014 benchmark levels and updated seasonal adjustment factors.

Table B-3. Average hourly and weekly earnings of all employees on private nonfarm payrolls by industry sector, seasonally adjusted

Industry	Average hourly earnings				Average weekly earnings			
	Feb. 2014	Dec. 2014	Jan. 2015ᵖ	Feb. 2015ᵖ	Feb. 2014	Dec. 2014	Jan. 2015ᵖ	Feb. 2015ᵖ
Total private..	$24.30	$24.62	$24.75	$24.78	$835.92	$851.85	$856.35	$857.39
Goods-producing.......................................	25.57	25.77	25.88	25.90	1,030.47	1,046.26	1,048.14	1,054.13
Mining and logging..................................	30.74	30.70	30.66	30.73	1,386.37	1,378.43	1,370.50	1,370.56
Construction...	26.55	26.81	26.98	26.91	1,022.18	1,050.95	1,052.22	1,065.64
Manufacturing..	24.70	24.87	24.97	25.01	1,007.76	1,017.18	1,023.77	1,025.41
Durable goods.....................................	26.12	26.21	26.28	26.37	1,078.76	1,085.09	1,090.62	1,091.72
Nondurable goods................................	22.23	22.49	22.62	22.60	889.20	904.10	909.32	910.78
Private service-providing.............................	23.99	24.34	24.48	24.52	796.47	812.96	817.63	818.97
Trade, transportation, and utilities................	21.27	21.49	21.64	21.66	729.56	743.55	748.74	749.44
Wholesale trade...................................	27.93	28.19	28.37	28.32	1,080.89	1,096.59	1,103.59	1,101.65
Retail trade..	16.85	17.12	17.32	17.33	524.04	537.57	543.85	544.16
Transportation and warehousing..............	22.79	22.88	22.84	22.94	879.69	892.32	886.19	892.37
Utilities..	35.90	35.94	36.05	36.42	1,514.98	1,516.67	1,524.92	1,536.92
Information...	33.42	34.35	34.40	34.47	1,229.86	1,246.91	1,255.60	1,258.16
Financial activities..................................	30.48	31.05	31.18	31.27	1,133.86	1,161.27	1,166.13	1,169.50
Professional and business services.............	29.04	29.48	29.74	29.78	1,048.34	1,070.12	1,076.59	1,078.04
Education and health services....................	24.57	24.90	25.02	25.04	803.44	814.23	820.66	821.31
Leisure and hospitality.............................	13.79	14.10	14.17	14.23	359.92	370.83	374.09	375.67
Other services.......................................	21.77	22.17	22.25	22.30	690.11	705.01	709.78	711.37

p Preliminary

NOTE: Data have been revised to reflect March 2014 benchmark levels and updated seasonal adjustment factors.

Table B-4. Indexes of aggregate weekly hours and payrolls for all employees on private nonfarm payrolls by industry sector, seasonally adjusted
[2007=100]

Industry	Index of aggregate weekly hours[1]					Index of aggregate weekly payrolls[2]				
	Feb. 2014	Dec. 2014	Jan. 2015ᵖ	Feb. 2015ᵖ	Percent change from: Jan. 2015 - Feb. 2015ᵖ	Feb. 2014	Dec. 2014	Jan. 2015ᵖ	Feb. 2015ᵖ	Percent change from: Jan. 2015 - Feb. 2015ᵖ
Total private.....................................	99.8	102.7	102.9	103.1	0.2	115.7	120.6	121.5	121.9	0.3
Goods-producing............................	87.4	90.1	90.2	90.8	0.7	101.0	105.0	105.5	106.3	0.8
Mining and logging........................	124.3	128.8	127.4	126.0	-1.1	153.4	158.8	156.8	155.4	-0.9
Construction.................................	80.1	84.8	85.0	86.7	2.0	92.3	98.8	99.7	101.4	1.7
Manufacturing..............................	89.0	90.5	90.9	90.9	0.0	102.2	104.7	105.5	105.8	0.3
Durable goods...........................	88.5	90.7	91.1	91.0	-0.1	102.7	105.6	106.3	106.6	0.3
Nondurable goods......................	90.0	90.7	90.8	90.9	0.1	101.5	103.5	104.2	104.3	0.1
Private service-providing....................	103.0	106.0	106.2	106.5	0.3	119.8	125.1	126.1	126.6	0.4
Trade, transportation, and utilities.......	97.5	100.4	100.5	100.8	0.3	111.6	116.1	117.1	117.5	0.3
Wholesale trade.........................	97.7	99.7	100.0	100.2	0.2	113.9	117.3	118.3	118.4	0.1
Retail trade..............................	96.3	98.8	99.0	99.2	0.2	107.2	111.9	113.4	113.7	0.3
Transportation and warehousing......	100.9	105.8	105.2	105.9	0.7	116.7	122.8	122.0	123.3	1.1
Utilities...................................	100.3	101.9	102.2	102.0	-0.2	118.9	121.0	121.7	122.8	0.9
Information.................................	91.4	91.7	92.4	92.6	0.2	108.8	112.2	113.2	113.7	0.4
Financial activities.........................	96.6	98.6	98.9	99.0	0.1	114.9	119.4	120.2	120.7	0.4
Professional and business services.....	107.0	111.0	110.7	111.0	0.3	125.9	132.6	133.4	133.9	0.4
Education and health services...........	111.7	114.0	114.6	114.9	0.3	129.3	133.7	135.0	135.5	0.4
Leisure and hospitality....................	108.2	112.2	112.9	113.4	0.4	120.4	127.6	129.1	130.2	0.9
Other services.............................	97.3	98.9	99.3	99.5	0.2	120.2	124.4	125.4	125.9	0.4

[1] The indexes of aggregate weekly hours are calculated by dividing the current month's estimates of aggregate hours by the corresponding 2007 annual average aggregate hours. Aggregate hours estimates are the product of estimates of average weekly hours and employment.

[2] The indexes of aggregate weekly payrolls are calculated by dividing the current month's estimates of aggregate weekly payrolls by the corresponding 2007 annual average aggregate weekly payrolls. Aggregate payrolls estimates are the product of estimates of average hourly earnings, average weekly hours, and employment.

p Preliminary

NOTE: Data have been revised to reflect March 2014 benchmark levels and updated seasonal adjustment factors.

Table B-5. Employment of women on nonfarm payrolls by industry sector, seasonally adjusted

Industry	Women employees (in thousands)				Percent of all employees			
	Feb. 2014	Dec. 2014	Jan. 2015[P]	Feb. 2015[P]	Feb. 2014	Dec. 2014	Jan. 2015[P]	Feb. 2015[P]
Total nonfarm..	68,062	69,330	69,413	69,575	49.4	49.3	49.3	49.3
Total private..	55,608	56,809	56,893	57,044	47.9	47.9	47.8	47.8
Goods-producing..................................	4,171	4,265	4,269	4,270	21.9	21.9	21.8	21.8
Mining and logging.............................	115	123	123	123	13.1	13.5	13.6	13.7
Construction......................................	763	796	799	799	12.6	12.7	12.6	12.6
Manufacturing....................................	3,293	3,346	3,347	3,348	27.2	27.2	27.2	27.2
Durable goods................................	1,754	1,798	1,804	1,807	23.0	23.1	23.1	23.1
Nondurable goods...........................	1,539	1,548	1,543	1,541	34.1	34.3	34.1	34.1
Private service-providing..........................	51,437	52,544	52,624	52,774	53.0	53.0	53.0	53.0
Trade, transportation, and utilities.............	10,594	10,780	10,802	10,839	40.5	40.4	40.4	40.5
Wholesale trade..............................	1,715.2	1,715.0	1,718.5	1,728.3	29.6	29.2	29.2	29.3
Retail trade.....................................	7,668.3	7,816.5	7,830.7	7,852.1	50.3	50.4	50.4	50.5
Transportation and warehousing.............	1,076.2	1,114.0	1,118.3	1,124.6	23.6	23.5	23.6	23.6
Utilities..	134.1	134.1	134.2	133.6	24.4	24.0	24.0	23.9
Information.......................................	1,090	1,112	1,115	1,117	40.1	40.2	40.2	40.2
Financial activities..............................	4,558	4,611	4,615	4,615	57.5	57.3	57.2	57.1
Professional and business services...........	8,408	8,658	8,648	8,671	44.6	44.5	44.5	44.5
Education and health services.................	16,341	16,695	16,729	16,777	76.8	76.9	76.9	76.9
Leisure and hospitality.........................	7,554	7,750	7,773	7,814	52.0	51.8	51.9	51.9
Other services...................................	2,892	2,938	2,942	2,941	52.2	52.4	52.4	52.3
Government...	12,454	12,521	12,520	12,531	57.1	57.2	57.2	57.2

p Preliminary

NOTE: Data have been revised to reflect March 2014 benchmark levels and updated seasonal adjustment factors.

ESTABLISHMENT DATA

Table B-6. Employment of production and nonsupervisory employees on private nonfarm payrolls by industry sector, seasonally adjusted[1]

[In thousands]

Industry	Feb. 2014	Dec. 2014	Jan. 2015[p]	Feb. 2015[p]
Total private...	95,860	97,923	98,086	98,339
Goods-producing..	13,721	14,051	14,102	14,138
Mining and logging..	645	669	664	660
Construction...	4,564	4,719	4,760	4,792
Manufacturing...	8,512	8,663	8,678	8,686
Durable goods...	5,241	5,361	5,372	5,382
Nondurable goods...	3,271	3,302	3,306	3,304
Private service-providing...	82,139	83,872	83,984	84,201
Trade, transportation, and utilities..............................	22,108	22,478	22,499	22,571
Wholesale trade...	4,674.0	4,740.9	4,749.2	4,760.5
Retail trade...	13,039.8	13,186.9	13,200.8	13,240.0
Transportation and warehousing.............................	3,949.2	4,100.2	4,099.3	4,120.4
Utilities..	444.9	450.0	449.8	449.6
Information..	2,203	2,245	2,250	2,256
Financial activities...	6,114	6,213	6,227	6,234
Professional and business services............................	15,602	16,025	16,039	16,063
Education and health services..................................	18,688	19,069	19,105	19,152
Leisure and hospitality...	12,813	13,172	13,189	13,247
Other services..	4,611	4,670	4,675	4,678

[1] Data relate to production employees in mining and logging and manufacturing, construction employees in construction, and nonsupervisory employees in the service-providing industries. These groups account for approximately four-fifths of the total employment on private nonfarm payrolls.

p Preliminary

NOTE: Data have been revised to reflect March 2014 benchmark levels and updated seasonal adjustment factors.

Table B-7. Average weekly hours and overtime of production and nonsupervisory employees on private nonfarm payrolls by industry sector, seasonally adjusted[1]

Industry	Feb. 2014	Dec. 2014	Jan. 2015[p]	Feb. 2015[p]
AVERAGE WEEKLY HOURS				
Total private...	33.5	33.8	33.8	33.8
Goods-producing..	40.9	41.6	41.4	41.5
Mining and logging..	47.5	47.6	46.8	46.7
Construction...	38.6	39.9	39.4	40.0
Manufacturing..	41.6	42.1	42.1	42.0
Durable goods...	42.1	42.4	42.4	42.3
Nondurable goods...	40.9	41.6	41.5	41.5
Private service-providing.......................................	32.3	32.5	32.5	32.5
Trade, transportation, and utilities...........................	33.3	33.9	33.7	33.8
Wholesale trade..	38.5	38.6	38.7	38.7
Retail trade...	29.7	30.3	30.1	30.2
Transportation and warehousing...........................	38.2	39.0	38.3	38.7
Utilities..	42.2	42.2	42.2	42.0
Information...	36.0	35.8	36.0	36.0
Financial activities..	36.6	36.8	36.8	36.9
Professional and business services.........................	35.4	35.7	35.6	35.6
Education and health services...............................	31.9	32.0	32.1	32.0
Leisure and hospitality..	25.1	25.2	25.2	25.3
Other services...	30.6	30.8	30.7	30.8
AVERAGE OVERTIME HOURS				
Manufacturing..	4.3	4.6	4.4	4.3
Durable goods..	4.5	4.7	4.4	4.3
Nondurable goods..	4.1	4.4	4.4	4.4

[1] Data relate to production employees in mining and logging and manufacturing, construction employees in construction, and nonsupervisory employees in the service-providing industries. These groups account for approximately four-fifths of the total employment on private nonfarm payrolls.

p Preliminary

NOTE: Data have been revised to reflect March 2014 benchmark levels and updated seasonal adjustment factors.

ESTABLISHMENT DATA
Table B-8. Average hourly and weekly earnings of production and nonsupervisory employees on private nonfarm payrolls by industry sector, seasonally adjusted[1]

Industry	Average hourly earnings				Average weekly earnings			
	Feb. 2014	Dec. 2014	Jan. 2015[p]	Feb. 2015[p]	Feb. 2014	Dec. 2014	Jan. 2015[p]	Feb. 2015[p]
Total private..	$20.48	$20.72	$20.80	$20.80	$686.08	$700.34	$703.04	$703.04
Goods-producing.......................................	21.46	21.66	21.72	21.70	877.71	901.06	899.21	900.55
Mining and logging.................................	26.71	26.63	26.60	26.33	1,268.73	1,267.59	1,244.88	1,229.61
Construction...	24.55	24.78	24.90	24.76	947.63	988.72	981.06	990.40
Manufacturing.......................................	19.48	19.62	19.67	19.69	810.37	826.00	828.11	826.98
Durable goods....................................	20.56	20.69	20.72	20.78	865.58	877.26	878.53	878.99
Nondurable goods...............................	17.68	17.86	17.92	17.90	723.11	742.98	743.68	742.85
Private service-providing............................	20.27	20.52	20.61	20.61	654.72	666.90	669.83	669.83
Trade, transportation, and utilities................	18.12	18.36	18.48	18.47	603.40	622.40	622.78	624.29
Wholesale trade..................................	23.09	23.31	23.36	23.31	888.97	899.77	904.03	902.10
Retail trade..	14.25	14.43	14.65	14.65	423.23	437.23	440.97	442.43
Transportation and warehousing...............	20.30	20.74	20.71	20.68	775.46	808.86	793.19	800.32
Utilities...	32.95	33.16	33.10	33.45	1,390.49	1,399.35	1,396.82	1,404.90
Information..	28.66	28.46	28.40	28.45	1,031.76	1,018.87	1,022.40	1,024.20
Financial activities..................................	24.42	25.00	25.08	25.15	893.77	920.00	922.94	928.04
Professional and business services.............	24.19	24.32	24.42	24.43	856.33	868.22	869.35	869.71
Education and health services....................	21.54	21.83	21.90	21.93	687.13	698.56	702.99	701.76
Leisure and hospitality............................	11.95	12.29	12.30	12.32	299.95	309.71	309.96	311.70
Other services......................................	18.39	18.71	18.78	18.82	562.73	576.27	576.55	579.66

[1] Data relate to production employees in mining and logging and manufacturing, construction employees in construction, and nonsupervisory employees in the service-providing industries. These groups account for approximately four-fifths of the total employment on private nonfarm payrolls.

p Preliminary

NOTE: Data have been revised to reflect March 2014 benchmark levels and updated seasonal adjustment factors.

Table B-9. Indexes of aggregate weekly hours and payrolls for production and nonsupervisory employees on private nonfarm payrolls by industry sector, seasonally adjusted[1]

[2002=100]

Industry	Index of aggregate weekly hours[2]					Index of aggregate weekly payrolls[3]				
	Feb. 2014	Dec. 2014	Jan. 2015ᴾ	Feb. 2015ᴾ	Percent change from: Jan. 2015 - Feb. 2015ᴾ	Feb. 2014	Dec. 2014	Jan. 2015ᴾ	Feb. 2015ᴾ	Percent change from: Jan. 2015 - Feb. 2015ᴾ
Total private....................................	107.0	110.3	110.5	110.8	0.3	146.5	152.7	153.6	154.0	0.3
Goods-producing.............................	85.8	89.3	89.2	89.7	0.6	112.7	118.5	118.7	119.1	0.3
Mining and logging.........................	162.8	169.2	165.1	163.8	-0.8	252.9	262.1	255.5	250.8	-1.8
Construction................................	88.2	94.3	93.9	96.0	2.2	116.9	126.1	126.3	128.3	1.6
Manufacturing..............................	81.3	83.7	83.9	83.7	-0.2	103.6	107.4	107.9	107.8	-0.1
Durable goods...........................	82.9	85.4	85.6	85.5	-0.1	106.4	110.3	110.7	111.0	0.3
Nondurable goods......................	78.8	80.9	80.8	80.8	0.0	98.5	102.1	102.4	102.2	-0.2
Private service-providing....................	113.0	116.1	116.3	116.6	0.3	157.1	163.4	164.3	164.7	0.2
Trade, transportation, and utilities.......	102.6	106.2	105.7	106.4	0.7	132.7	139.1	139.3	140.1	0.6
Wholesale trade.........................	106.0	107.8	108.2	108.5	0.3	144.1	148.0	148.9	149.0	0.1
Retail trade.............................	98.0	101.1	100.6	101.2	0.6	119.7	125.1	126.3	127.1	0.6
Transportation and warehousing......	113.6	120.4	118.2	120.0	1.5	146.2	158.4	155.3	157.5	1.4
Utilities....................................	96.0	97.1	97.1	96.6	-0.5	132.1	134.4	134.1	134.8	0.5
Information.................................	90.5	91.7	92.4	92.7	0.3	128.4	129.2	130.0	130.6	0.5
Financial activities........................	105.3	107.6	107.9	108.3	0.4	158.3	165.5	166.5	167.6	0.7
Professional and business services.....	123.8	128.2	128.0	128.2	0.2	178.2	185.6	186.0	186.3	0.2
Education and health services...........	127.2	130.2	130.9	130.8	-0.1	180.8	187.6	189.1	189.3	0.1
Leisure and hospitality....................	117.8	121.6	121.7	122.8	0.9	159.9	169.7	170.1	171.8	1.0
Other services.............................	99.0	100.9	100.7	101.0	0.3	132.6	137.5	137.7	138.6	0.7

[1] Data relate to production employees in mining and logging and manufacturing, construction employees in construction, and nonsupervisory employees in the service-providing industries. These groups account for approximately four-fifths of the total employment on private nonfarm payrolls.

[2] The indexes of aggregate weekly hours are calculated by dividing the current month's estimates of aggregate hours by the corresponding 2002 annual average aggregate hours. Aggregate hours estimates are the product of estimates of average weekly hours and employment.

[3] The indexes of aggregate weekly payrolls are calculated by dividing the current month's estimates of aggregate weekly payrolls by the corresponding 2002 annual average aggregate weekly payrolls. Aggregate payrolls estimates are the product of estimates of average hourly earnings, average weekly hours, and employment.

p Preliminary

NOTE: Data have been revised to reflect March 2014 benchmark levels and updated seasonal adjustment factors.